Here Am I, Lord...

Please Send Someone Else!

CYNTHIA A. ALLAN

Ahuas Emigré Press
BROOKLINE, MA
www.ahuasemigre.com

24 23 22 21 20 19 18 17 16 15   7 6 5 4 3 2

First edition: 21 December 2005
Second edition: 3 September 2016

Ahuas Emigré Press, Brookline, MA
http://ahuasemigre.com
C. Scott Ananian, editor

He will cover you with his feathers,
    and under his wings you will find refuge;
    his faithfulness will be your shield and rampart.

Psalm 91:4

But as for me, it is good to be near God.
    I have made the Sovereign Lord my refuge;
    I will tell of all your deeds.

Psalm 73:28

Contents

CONTENTS

Seventeen pages of photographs appear on pages 113–129.

The Book of Life

Shortly after I had come to accept the Lord as my Savior, something out of the ordinary, something mysterious and unexplainable, happened. I was seventeen years old, full of the newness of my spiritual life. My Bible was with me wherever I went, including the halls of my high school where, I think, I might have been using it more as a "badge" of my righteousness than as a point of reference. My mother was offering money to any of my friends who could get me off of this "religious kick."

It was a warm spring night. I had finished my homework and I was tired. It was late and time for bed. The house was quiet, and I was soon fast asleep. But some time in the middle of the night I was awakened by a loud, droning sound that was coming from the direction of my window. I sensed the room was full of light but my body was facing away from the source. I struggled in vain to move, to roll over, to discover what was making the Sound or the Light, but I couldn't.

The Sound continued to move closer to the side of my bed and, as hard as I tried to move, I was frozen. Then the Sound suddenly stopped. The room was profoundly quiet. I was free to move, as if released from chains. I quickly rolled over to see what "presence" was in my room.

On the edge of my bed was a book: a large, thick book. The book was glowing with a light of its own. I sensed, though did not see, a being just outside the light of the book. The book was opened to a page. There were two columns of writing on the page. I began to read the words and realized that what I was reading was the story of my life, everything that would happen to me, the triumphs, the hurts, the mistakes, but most importantly there were words on the page telling what I needed to know for my life. As I read the words I knew they were very important but I wouldn't be able to remember them unless I could read them a second time. The urgency of reading those words was propelled by the knowledge of a time limit. I raced down the page, devouring the writing. As I read the last word my eyes leaped back to the beginning. I HAD to read it a second time, to remember it! But as soon as my eyes retouched the first word, the droning noise started anew, and I was paralyzed, unable to move my eyes or head in any direction.

The book closed. The glowing light surrounding the book slowly drifted toward the window and the noise faded as if into a tunnel. When the room was completely dark I was able to move again. I was perplexed, bewildered, and amazed, but not afraid. Something fantastic had just happened but to this day, 30 years later, I am not sure why.

Was it a dream? Common sense would say yes. But even as a dream there was an importance and vividness to the image that I have never experienced since.

Someday, I know I will see that book again. And my Lord will be standing beside me as we view it together. He will explain it then. And I will see that every event, every incident, every crisis and joy had been written in that book long before it occurred, by an Author who cared deeply and was close with me every step of the way.

All the days ordained for me
were written in your book
before one of them came to be.

How precious to me are your thoughts, O God!
How vast is the sum of them!   Psalm 139:16–17

* * *

The book now in your hands contains some of the things my seventeen-year-old self must have read that night: stories about the joys God has brought me, and tales of my struggles with Him. I can look back now at the open part of my life's book and share it with you: what God has taught, and the lessons I have still to learn...

PART I

Single Mom: Not What I Had Planned!

CHAPTER 1

Why Do We Need Jesus?

I'd always found church to be a profitable experience. My mother directed a choir in a neighboring town, but each Sunday morning she made sure my brother and I were dutifully dropped off at the door of the First Congregational Church. My brother, who was eight years older than me and in his early teens, had no intention of spending time in Sunday School. And I, being the typical younger sister, threatened that I would tell Mom and Dad if he didn't. So a deal was made: he gave me his offering money, and I wouldn't squeal. Yes, church was truly a profitable experience!

I was a child of the fifties. The memory of World War II was fresh in everyone's mind. The "Cold War" was a strong reality. The neighbors across the street had the finest bomb shelter in the neighborhood. The woman had enough food put aside in her basement to last three years. There were beds, water barrels, blankets, a radio, emergency lamps, and blackout curtains. They were the envy of the town.

Popular Mechanics regularly had instructions in their issues for building your own backyard underground bomb shelter. I used to cut them out and put them on my father's workbench, trying to leave a gentle hint for our future safety. And every month our school had its civil defense drill. We would all pile down into the school basement and crowd around the boiler. Thinking back, this probably was not the best place to be if a bomb hit: I certainly wouldn't want to be hugging a boiler in such a situation.

Even the *Weekly Reader,* the children's current-events newspaper, did its part to instill in each child the looming threat of ATOMIC WAR. In one memorable issue there was an aerial view of New York City with a giant bull's-eye drawn on it. Inside each circle was the time it would take a person to DIE if the bomb hit the center of the city. The first two circles would be killed instantly on impact. My town, which was eight miles from New York City, was in the fifth circle. We would be dead in ten minutes! With such a constant barrage of impending doom, I had come to the conclusion that I probably would not live a long life and if I reached twenty I'd be lucky.

Religious matters and eternity floated in and out of my awareness. The Congregational Church was a very social church. The minister did a fine job preaching what each person's civic duty should be and what we all OUGHT to do. He was great at preaching "The Oughts"! But I don't ever remember hearing the WHYS. God was presented as a wonderful old man sitting up in heaven nodding his head benevolently as he watched his children below. He was All-Knowing, All-Seeing, All-Caring, and All-Loving. He was a delightful being. Jesus was occasionally mentioned, especially at Christmas time, when we all knew him to be the baby in the manger. We would also hear his name mentioned at Easter. How he and the Easter Bunny were related I wasn't quite sure.

As I became a teenager I started questioning the need for a Jesus. Why did Christianity have TWO gods? If God were All-Loving and All-Caring, why did we need a Jesus? What was his purpose? From the way the minister presented it, God seemed to have things pretty well under control. WHAT PURPOSE DID JESUS HAVE? This became a dominant question in my mind. I felt *compelled* to find an answer. Who could I ask? Mom and Dad didn't seem a good source of such information. Mom could sing me every hymn that mentioned Jesus but her understanding stopped there. Dad—well, Dad just wasn't into religion. He took Sunday to be a "day of rest," literally, and did his part by resting the entire day. So I decided to ask my Sunday School teachers. I didn't find a satisfying answer there. I then asked the youth counselor at church. She didn't have an answer, either, but she suggested I make an appointment with the minister and ask him. So I did just that. As I sat in front of him, the room was positively stuffed with the importance and weight of his position. He was a large man and his sigh resonated deeply as he asked me why I had come to see him. Not wanting to waste his time I got right to the point and voiced my question: "Why do we need Jesus? What purpose does he have for us?"

He leaned back in his chair and, tired, looked at me. "How old are you?" he asked.

"Sixteen, sir. I will be seventeen pretty soon."

"You have a brother, don't you? He was a bit of a problem a while back," he queried.

"Yes, sir," remembering my brother's wilder years as a teenager.

6

"But he enlisted in the army, and is married now and doing just fine," I defended.

Oblivious, the minister was still ponderously considering something. "You've had many things to worry about in your life. I suggest you not worry about this question. You are too young for these matters." With these weighty words of wisdom delivered, he dismissed me.

I still did not have an answer to my question.

My sister Dea, who was thirteen years older than me and married, was going through a similar period of questioning. She had three small boys and a husband, who was ambitious and demanding. Looking for some meaning in the chaos and confusion of life she had started attending a small non-denominational church. The church was firmly rooted in the Bible and she came face to face with the person of Jesus Christ. She took Him as her Savior and claimed the promise in Acts 16:31:

> *Believe in the Lord Jesus, and you will be saved—you and your household.*

The household she claimed included not only her children and husband, but us: her sister and brother and mother and father.

My brother, the rebellious teenager, the one who couldn't stand to go to Sunday School, the one who financed a good part of my childhood, was the first to come into the fold. He accepted the Lord as His Savior when a friend was carted off to jail. Life's options became crystal clear to him and he accepted Jesus as Lord.

I was still groping around for an answer to my question. On Easter Sunday, the whole family went to Dea's church: Mom and Dad, my brother and his wife, my sister's husband and boys, and me. *This* pastor did not preach about the nice old man sitting up in heaven who nodded his head kindly at his children below. He didn't preach about the social *do*s and *don't*s in society. This Pastor preached about a RIGHTEOUS God, a HOLY God and about SIN. SIN that was a barrier between God and his creation. Sin was not measured in QUANTITY but in FACT. We sinned by our very nature. From the time of Adam and Eve we have worshiped ourselves, served ourselves, put ourselves before all else, even before God. And even our "deeds of righteousness" were vain acts to elevate ourselves above others.

All our righteous acts are like filthy rags.

Isaiah 64:6

God, by His very nature of Holiness, cannot let into His presence SIN. But His love and compassion are real. They exist because He sent His Son, His own being, to pay the penalty of damnation in our place. The REASON for Jesus is the ransom he paid, a ransom in pain and suffering beyond our comprehension, that he endured for us so that we could once again enjoy the fellowship of the Loving Father of Creation. The proof that he paid that ransom was his resurrection. The empty tomb was a sign for all to see that there is now no more condemnation before God for all that believe and have looked to Jesus as their atonement.

These were the words I heard that Sunday. Words that moved me so deeply that I could do nothing but cry. I cried for my own sin. I cried for my lack of understanding. I cried for the helplessness of all mankind, and I cried for the disregard I had had for the supreme atonement embodied in Jesus Christ.

I was trapped in the unbearable weight of my new understanding and had not yet found the release.

We returned to my sister's home after church. I was still an emotional wreck, crying every time I attempted to internally pray. My mother was wringing her hands in concern but I couldn't find the words to explain. My sister was busy getting the Easter dinner on the table. My father was satisfied with himself, having been to church already *two* times this year, filling his yearly quota when it was only April. The little boys were running around the house making their own chaos.

I felt a gentle touch on my arm. "Cyndy, do you want to pray with me?" my brother quietly asked.

My brother, who had teased me, tormented me, and hassled me as we grew up, was about to show me God's wonderful grace. "Yes," I meekly responded.

We went into another room and he knelt down beside me and took my hand. "Father, forgive us. Forgive us for the sins we do, for the things we don't understand, for the times we have lived so far away from you. Father, I put my little sister before you and ask you to show her your love and presence. Fill her with your Spirit. Give to her this day, your salvation. Cleanse her and renew her with the understanding that you alone can give," he prayed.

8

In a rush of divine grace I felt the presence of God, standing with his arms lovingly around my brother and me. All else in the world had hushed. I was at His altar and I cried as a small child who has been lost and finds her father. "God, forgive me. I am so sorry for all I have done. I am sorry for not understanding. Lord, Jesus, be my Savior and my Lord. I do not understand everything even now but I know I need you. Please, Lord, come to me."

That feeling of release and joy is beyond expression. God enveloped me with divine compassion that reached deep into my soul's inmost realms. He was my Lord and I—was His child. I was born anew in Spirit. Yes, I acknowledged gratefully, there *is* a need for Jesus. He is the Lamb of God.

> *For all have sinned and fall short of the glory of God and are justified freely by his grace through the redemption that came by Christ Jesus. God presented him as an atonement, through faith in his blood.*   Romans 3:23–24

CHAPTER 2

Does It Really Matter?

Graduation from high school was only two weeks away, and I was studying diligently for final exams. The phone rang but I had no intention of answering it.

"Cyndy," my mother yelled up to me. "The telephone—it's for you."

I picked up the upstairs extension. "Hello?"

"Is this the residence of Cyndy Allan?" asked a male voice I didn't immediately recognize.

"Yes," I answered hesitantly.

"This is the National Ajax Quiz Show," the voice exclaimed. "You win a prize if you can guess the name of the person on the other end of this line!"

The voice sounded vaguely familiar. Who could it be? I knew it was *not* an Ajax Contest. But who was it? I started quickly going through boys' names in my class, alphabetically. I didn't have far to go.

"Cliff?" I said.

"You win! You win!" the voice excitedly proclaimed.

"What did I win?" I asked

"All the answers on tomorrow's humanities exam if you will go out with me this Saturday."

Cliff...Cliff was in the "enriched" track in our school, the track reserved for the smartest and ablest in our class. He was both of those and also "tall, dark, and handsome." I had known him since first grade. His mother and mine, both having names ending in "A," were class mothers together. His mother made him wear green shoelaces! I remembered how shy he was. He ran for student counsel president. Johnny Beacher did most of the speeches for him, but he won. We were both in band and orchestra together. He played the trumpet quite well, with his head slightly tilted to one side. I played the viola and clarinet not quite so well, tilted or otherwise. Did I hear him right? Was he really asking me out on a date?

"Where would we go?" I said, to confirm that he had actually asked me out.

"How about to a movie? Johnny and Nancy want to see *Goldfinger* and you and I could join them," he said.

"Okay," I said calmly, to hide the fact that my heart was racing two hundred miles an hour. I was going out on a date with Cliff Ananian!

That was the first of many dates that summer. We kept it casual. We were both going away to college in the fall. I was going to Ohio University in Athens, and he was going to the Massachusetts Institute of Technology in Cambridge. It was not a time to get serious.

But nightly, when I would leave my job at Bambergers, he would be leaning against a pillar, waiting for me. He always pretended he had just been strolling by and was surprised to see me. But he *had* been waiting.

We went to the shore in the summer. We strolled along the boardwalk and watched the barkers call people to their games. Cliff put down his money only once, on a dart game. He threw three darts and won a large spotted dog which he gave to me. I called the dog "Evol," love spelled backward. But we had not declared any such lasting sentiment openly.

My sister took me aside one day. "Cyndy, I am concerned about your dating Cliff."

"Why?" I demanded. "What's wrong with Cliff?"

"Oh, Cyndy, he's a wonderful boy. I like him very much. But the Bible tells believers not to be yoked with non-believers. Does he know the Lord?"

"No, but hey, we're just friends! It doesn't really matter. We haven't made any plans to get married or anything like that. Don't worry, Dea. We're just friends," I explained.

"Friends can easily turn into something more," she said.

In the fall we parted as *good* friends who gave each other the freedom to date others. But I missed him...

In February the dorm phone rang at midnight. My name was called down the hall. "Call for Cyndy Allan! Cyndy Allan! Call for Cyndy Allan!"

"Hello," I answered groggily. I had been in a sound sleep and couldn't imagine who this could be.

"Cyndy, this is Cliff. I'm freezing to death! I was trying to come and see you. I've been hitchhiking since four o'clock this morning and

I've gotten as far as Lancaster, Ohio. But no car or truck has passed in the last two hours. Is there any way you can come and get me?"

"Where are you right now?" I asked.

"In a phone booth," he shot back flippantly.

"Yes, but where is the phone booth?" I insisted.

"On Route 33, just south of Lancaster," he responded.

"Cliff, I don't know how I am going to get you. It's past curfew. I will have to get permission to leave the dorm and then I'll have to find someone who has a car. But I'll do it. I just don't know how yet. But I'll find a way. Give me the phone number of the booth. I will call you back in ten minutes."

Lancaster was forty miles north of Athens. The boyfriend of a friend volunteered to drive me. The dorm's Resident Assistant gave me permission to leave. One hour later I picked up a very cold and tired Cliff. It was so good to see him, so good to hold him. He had hitchhiked from Boston to Ohio with hardly a dime in his pocket, just to see me.

I transferred from Ohio University to Boston University a year later. My explanation was to cut down his "hitchhiking time" and to save him from freezing to death. But our relationship was different now. Friendship had grown into something more. The word "love" crept in. It spoke through his eyes. It came from my heart. It existed in the unspoken moments between us. All around us the turbulence of the late sixties raged: anti-Vietnam demonstrations, riots, the emergence of the Hippies, and drugs. The world seemed to be a whirling dervish. But he steadied my world.

I felt safe with him. And I loved him.

"Is he a believer?" my sister would ask.

"No, Dea, not yet. But he's my best friend. Does it really matter if he doesn't know the Lord? He's such a good person," I rationalized.

The following summer Cliff's fraternity brother gave him his 1937 Packard to babysit during July and August. The movie *Bonnie and Clyde* had just finished playing in the theaters. This car was perfect! It even had running boards on the side. We bought black water pistols and played Bonnie and Clyde as we cruised the streets of our town. We had mock fights with our friends and occasionally doused an innocent bystander with a misplaced squirt. It was a summer of carefree fun.

One evening, as we were leaving on a date in the Packard, the lights fuse blew. We were a mile from home and Cliff attempted to drive back for a replacement. We hadn't gotten a block when a police-man pulled us over for driving without headlights. He perfunctorily asked for driver's license and registration. The license was no prob-lem but Cliff tried to explain to the officer that he was babysitting the car for a friend and wasn't sure where the registration was.

"Try the glove compartment," the officer barked.

That sounded like a logical place to look, so I swung open the compartment, oblivious to its other contents as I rummaged around.

I heard the officer inhale sharply. "Freeze!" he shouted. "Get out of the car with your hands up!"

This was rather dramatic for a misplaced registration but we com-plied. "Don't move! I'm calling for back up. Keep your hands over the hood of the car! Don't move!" he repeated.

I was too scared to utter a word. Cliff was totally bewildered.

The officer picked up a stick from the ground and went back in the car on the passenger's side. Additional squad sirens were approaching. He opened the glove compartment again and placed the stick through some object he'd found there and carefully withdrew it. The other cars pulled in around him as he triumphantly held up the evidence. In the glare of the search lights it was plain to all that he was holding up a WATER PISTOL! The officer let it drop. "It's a toy!" he whimpered. He'd found the water guns we'd kept in the glove compartment.

"Caught them red-handed did ya, with a water pistol," joshed a fellow officer.

"Careful, you might get wet," added another.

The officer was mortified. The headline he was imagining—COP FROM SMALL TOWN NABS ARMED CAR THIEVES!—melted into the air. His moment of glory crashed into humiliation. We were escorted home by two squad cars—and the sound of laughter.

We were engaged that Christmas. Cliff gave me a blue elephant with a diamond ring around its trunk. I loved him dearly. Only my sister quietly admonished me. "Cyndy, is he a Christian? Is he a believer?"

"No, Dea, but he's such a good person. Does it really matter? He'll come to know the Lord, someday, I'm sure," I rationalized.

No one else was stressing this point so I buried it among the trivi-alities of life and the concerns of the present. Our relationship was so good. Did it really matter whether we shared the same commitment to God?

My cousin, Dotsy, was having a family reunion at her home in Vermont. My sister with her TEN children, and my cousin with her TEN children, my mother and father, my aunt and uncle, my brother and his family, my cousin, Freddy, and his family would all be there. Cliff and I were driving up together a bit later than the rest. In the six hours it took to get there we talked about many things, including religion and God.

"Cyndy, I don't believe that God cares one iota about what's happening on this planet. If there is a God it is the initial force of creation. But everything has been created, everything has been made. He has set the laws of nature to run the show. It's on auto-pilot. What happens down here now is up to us," he explained.

"No, Cliff, God is more than that. He's more than the rules of nature. He's a very personal God. He's deeply involved in the lives of those he has created. When we pray, he listens. When we cry, he cares. He wants each of his children to have an intimate fellowship with Him. We can't, though, as long as we hold onto the sin in our lives and our selfish ambitions. We can't hear his voice or know his touch. Only when we lay it all down and ask Him to forgive us, ask Jesus to intercede, and we *accept* the atonement He has already made for us, can we have that intimate relationship with God our Father. He loves each of us, more than we can understand."

Cliff stubbornly held onto his position that God—if there was a God—was the force of creation and did *not* enter into the lives of individuals. I argued that He *did!* We were deeply engrossed in the discussion and did not notice the miles speed by. We were on the Thruway to Vermont, and I was driving. The interchange for the next major artery came up quickly. I veered off, still traveling above 60 miles an hour and realizing too late that the road I was now on was under construction. A large concrete pillar, placed in preparation for a bridge overpass, was directly in front of us. Only a small yellow blinker warned of the danger. I had no time to stop and no way to avoid the imminent impact.

"Oh God, help!" I desperately implored.

Cliff, sitting beside me, was as white as a sheet, braced for the inevitable.

Then—the steering wheel began moving on its own. The car came to a stop, parallel to the concrete pillar. There were no screeching brakes, no wild swerves. The car just stopped—as if picked up and checked by a Higher Force.

I was crying, thanking God for saving us.

Cliff got out of the car saying, "No! There is no way! We couldn't have done that!"

"Cliff, don't you see?" I tried to explain. "God was showing you that He is more than the forces of nature. He can even change those forces to spare individuals' lives—your life and my life. Look, Cliff. Look for yourself. There are no skid marks!"

"No, it can't be," he argued defensively. He refused to accept what seemed so clear to me.

God had broken through the very laws of momentum and gravity in order to show Cliff who He was, to show Cliff He cared, to show Cliff that his life was of importance to Him. Why couldn't Cliff see? Why couldn't he understand?

"Cyndy," my sister asked. "Is Cliff a believer? Does he know the Lord?"

"No Dea, not yet. But we have such a good relationship. Does it really matter? He's my best friend. And Dea, I love him so much. I'm sure he will know the Lord someday... someday, Dea..."

> *Do not be yoked together with unbelievers. For what do righteousness and wickedness have in common? Or what fellowship can light have with darkness? What harmony is there between Christ and Belial? What does a believer have in common with an unbeliever? What agreement is there between the temple of God and idols?* 2 Corinthians 6:14–16

CHAPTER 3

Knocking

Here I am! I stand at the door and knock. If anyone hears
my voice and opens the door, I will come in and eat with
him, and he with me.
                                                    Revelations 3:20

Cliff graduated with two degrees from MIT, and I graduated from
Boston University with a Masters degree in education. We were married August 6, 1972, in an Armenian Orthodox church. Cliff had insisted we be married in his family church rather than mine. He explained that his church was more than a religion. It was his heritage.
So I complied. The priest chanted the ceremony in Armenian. Gilded
crowns were placed on our heads and a golden cord wrapped around
us, symbolizing our eternal union. I knew without a doubt that this
was the man I wanted as my husband, and I loved him deeply.

How many ways can you love a person? How many things can
you love about someone? I loved him as a twenty-two-year-old loves:
idealistically, blindly, and passionately. He was my husband, he was
my best friend. He was sensitive and intelligent. He was someone I
could respect and trust.

Married life began in Spartanburg, South Carolina. Cliff was employed by an engineering firm, involved with research and development. I worked as a teacher in a school for emotionally-disturbed and
learning-disabled children. Life was full of challenges as both of us
embarked on our careers.

Cliff resolutely avoided issues of religion. He held to my father's
creed that Sunday was a day of rest and did his part by sleeping late and
avoiding all physical exertion. But God was not avoiding Cliff. His
Presence invisibly encircled him. I heard Him speak to him through
his friends. He listened to his dreams and his boasts. I was sure He
wept with him in disappointments. He cared about the things Cliff
cared about. He was waiting patiently for Cliff to allow him in.

God does not always knock on the doors of our lives among pro-
fundities. Sometimes it's in very simple ways, in common concerns.

One day we were returning to our car after a day of shopping, loaded down with bags and bundles and newly-acquired possessions. Cliff laid his wallet on top of the car as he fished for his keys. The car was unlocked, the bundles and bags shoved in helter-skelter, and we tumbled in as well. We were tired and glad to be heading home. The wallet, however, remained forgotten on the roof of the car.

An hour later Cliff realized that his wallet was missing. "Where could it be?" he moaned. He looked in every pocket, all over the house, all through the car. Where did he last have his wallet? Mentally he followed every step he'd made up to putting the wallet on the top of the car. Panic! That was the last place he'd remembered it. It could be anywhere now. All of his identification cards were in it, his credit cards, license and registration, and two hundred dollars in cash.

We got back in the car and slowly retraced our path to the center of Spartanburg, looking, searching frantically, hoping to spot the wallet as we went. We entered the same lot we had parked in an hour before. We scoured everywhere: under, around and over every car in the lot. There was no wallet to be seen. We were both frustrated and upset. How was he going to replace everything? What if someone used his credit cards to purchase thousands of dollars of merchandise? Where else could he look? What else could we do?

When we returned home he called a local radio station as a last resort, and asked them to announce the lost wallet over the air. A reward was offered. He could think of nothing more to do. And so we waited and waited for someone to respond.

"Cliff, you looked everywhere, you've tried everything. You even called the radio station and still nothing has turned up. The only thing you haven't done is pray. God cares about your wallet because He loves you and cares about you. Can't we ask God to help you find your wallet," I quietly suggested.

He was desperate! He took my hand without protest or belittling. Together we simply prayed for the wallet to be returned and closed our petition to God with a hushed and solemn, "Amen." Our "reverent" moment was shattered by the shrill ringing of the telephone.

"Hey, is this the home of Clifford...Cliff...Ani...?" a woman's voice asked in a heavy southern drawl.

"Yes," I answered, waiting for her to continue.

"I found his wallet and I'd like to give it back to him," the voice continued.

"You found his wallet!" I excitedly exclaimed. "That's wonderful! That's great! Thank you so much! Did you hear it announced over the radio?" I asked.

"No, my kids and me found it awhile ago, but we don't got no phone to call you on. Saw a phone here at the fire station and started thinking maybe I should call you," the lady explained.

"Is that where you are now?" I asked.

"Yes ma'am. You be wanting us to wait here for you?" she inquired.

"Yes, it will take us about twenty minutes to get there. Is that okay? We'll be there as fast as we can," I said.

"Ah huh. We'll be here, the kids and me."

Cliff was tremendously relieved to hear that his wallet had been found. We jumped into the car and started our third trip to the center of Spartanburg.

"I bet the money won't be in the wallet," Cliff said pessimistically.

"Cliff, if God has answered your prayer even the money will be accounted for," I optimistically assured him.

Moments later we pulled into the parking lot of the Spartanburg fire station. A woman with uncombed brown hair was standing there waiting for us. Two small barefoot children in dirty T-shirts were clutching her skirt. She walked toward us and handed the wallet to Cliff through the open window of the car.

"Thank you so much!" said Cliff as he quickly scanned through the wallet to see what was and wasn't there. All was present—except the money! Cliff shot me a look as if to say, "See!"

"Will you accept a reward?" he asked as he got out money from his pocket.

"Oh, no," said the woman. "We just wanted y'all to have your wallet back," and she walked away with the two children still clutching her.

As we drove home Cliff said, "I knew the money wouldn't be there. She probably took it out before she called us. You said, 'If God was in this even the money would still be in the wallet.' Well, the money wasn't there so God wasn't involved!"

"She looked like she could have used the two hundred dollars," I quietly reflected.

About eight the next morning the phone rang. Cliff had already left for work and I was almost out the door.

"Hey, uh... er... is Clifford Ann... Ani... is Clifford there?" asked an agitated male voice.

"No, I'm sorry but he's already left for work. Can I help you?" I said.

"Well, ah, hmm," hesitated the voice. "I guess you can. I think I'm losing my mind! I can't believe I'm doin' this. I had such a awful night last night. You see I was the one who done found your husband's wallet—me and my wife, that is. But I was the one that took the money. Doin' that don't usually bother me none. I mean—well anyway—last night I just couldn't sleep. Havin' that money plagued me all night. I can't tell you why but I just gotta give it back. I gotta give the money back to your husband, y'hear?"

The man had taken the money but he couldn't keep it, I mused. Yes, "if God were involved even the money would be accounted for," I had told Cliff. God *was* involved but it was Cliff that needed to be convinced.

"I'm going to give you my husband's work number. He'll be there by now. Call him and tell him exactly what you told me," I said.

That evening, when I asked him about the call, he told me the man had wanted to give back all the money. "He was pretty spooked about keeping it," he reflected.

"Why do you think he was so spooked?" I prodded.

"I sure don't know. It didn't make sense. He wasn't the kind of man that looked to be plagued by a conscience," he continued.

"Do you think maybe it was God that plagued him?" I suggested.

Cliff thought for awhile. "I can't say. Why would God care about money that belonged to me?"

"Because, silly, He's been trying to show you all these years that He loves you. He cares about every part of your life, even two hundred dollars that was lost in a wallet," I said. "Did you get the money back?"

"No," he said. "The man was really poor. I told him to keep the money and consider it a reward for finding the wallet. He needed it more than I did. See," he reflected, "I did something good for God. I gave money to the poor."

"That's only half of it," I whispered.

Jesus answered, "If you want to be perfect, go, sell your possessions and give to the poor, and you will have treasure in heaven. Then COME, FOLLOW ME." Matt. 19:21

Knock, knock, knock...
>   Do you hear?
>>   Do you see?
>>>   Will you follow?

CHAPTER 4

And a Child is Born

On September 27, 1976, our first son, Clifford Scott, was born. Cliff was so proud as he held his infant son.

"I want to be a good father to him," he said as he cradled him in his arms. "I want to be the kind of father he can look up to and respect. I want to be even a better father than my own dad was to me." His voice was filled with emotion as he said these words. Baby Scott held tightly to his father's finger, his little hand so tiny in his father's strong clasp. A whimper escaped. Protectively, Cliff placed his hand around Scott's small fist. "I won't let anything happen to you, son. I'll be there for you, always."

Cliff went on a buying spree to welcome his little boy home. He bought any- and everything that was blue. He stood in front of an array of stuffed animals: they were all too small, he decided. He finally made his selection, a dog—a brown dog—a *large* brown dog, four times the size of baby Scott. He called the dog Harvey and placed him in the crib. Fortunately Scott didn't take up much room yet. So Scott and Harvey coexisted in their small world for a time.

Sixteen months later our second son, Christopher Lee, was born. His entrance into the world was a bit louder and more demanding. He knew there was competition ahead and extra effort would be required. Cliff bought him a *large* gray bear for his crib. Cigars were passed out to everyone.

Cliff now had two sons to love and to guide, to protect and provide for. God had blessed him. They were healthy and intelligent. They grew and they adored him.

* * *

Scott was now two and Chris was toddling behind him. Christmas was approaching with all the excitement and commotion involved. Toys galore had been bought for the boys. The tree was buried behind a mountain of wrapped packages and bows. On Christmas Eve, true to his family's tradition, Cliff dressed up in the well-worn Santa Claus suit to play the part of the jolly old man. Grandma and Grandpa and

Cliff's brother, Uncle Steve, had joined us for the holiday. As Cliff entered the room, "ho-ho-hoing" and carrying a large sack over his shoulder, one-year-old Chris let out an ear-piercing wail: he wanted no part of this strange man! No gaily-adorned package could induce him to let go of my leg or take one step toward that scraggly-bearded bell-clanging stranger who had entered his house. Scott, however, had a smile on his face. "You look silly, Daddy," he said softly. He was not afraid of this man. He would know his daddy anywhere. He walked confidently toward "Santa Claus" and sat on his knee.

"Ho, ho, ho! And Scott, have you been a good boy this year?" chortled Santa Claus Cliff.

"Yes," smiled Scott, looking at me to make sure.

"And what did you want Santa Claus to bring you?" asked Cliff.

"A train," said Scott. "I want to be an engineer like you, Daddy."

Cliff smiled as he recognized Scott's confusion of the two meanings of "engineer."

"I hope not," he said. "You're going to be smart and make lots of money and will be your own boss," he prophesied. He handed Scott a large decorated box. It didn't take Scott long to discover the hoped-for train set, as well as a train engineer's hat, and a stuffed dog with a similar hat of its own. The dog was quickly named "Engineer Doggie," and was a bedtime favorite for years.

In church the bells were joyously ringing. Red poinsettias and pine wreaths hung by the windows. "This was the night," the pastor said, "that God gave the world the most precious gift of all, His son, Jesus Christ. It is the night that God established Peace, not peace as the world knows it, but Peace between God and man."

Forgiveness and fellowship again restored, through a baby born in a manger—who would grow up to die in our place because of the depth of God's love for us.

The people walking in darkness have seen a great light:
... For to us a child is born,
 to us a son is given,
 and the government will be on his shoulders.
And he will be called
 Wonderful Counselor, Mighty God,
 Everlasting Father, Prince of Peace.
         Isaiah 9:2,6

CHAPTER 5

Happy New Year

I couldn't settle down. I couldn't get to sleep. I paced towards the boys' room one more time. Scott's rhythmic breathing assured me he was sleeping soundly, but Chris was still awake. His cold had made him fretful. He was standing in his crib, now, rubbing his ears and crying softly.

"Poor little guy," I soothed as I picked him up. "You probably have another ear ache." I felt his forehead and it was warm. I cradled him closer to me as I moved in the rocking chair.

It was past midnight and Cliff still was not home. What was it tonight? I tried to remember: poker, racket ball, a night out with the guys, or another late night at the office? There had been so many different reasons lately, it was hard to keep track.

Chris whimpered again. I would have to take him to the doctor tomorrow and have his ears checked, I mused. I rocked him back and forth in the unlit room. Where could Cliff be? My mind ominously dreaded his absence. He had been so distant lately. What was wrong?

I heard the door open downstairs. Cliff's shoeless feet ascended the stairs. I put Chris back in his crib, hoping he'd stay asleep, and went into our bedroom. Cliff was trying to maneuver in the dark.

"You can turn on the light, Cliff. I'm not asleep," I said quietly behind him.

He turned in surprise. "You're still awake?" he asked.

"Chris has another ear infection. He's been crying a good part of the night. Where were you tonight?"

"I was playing poker with some of the guys," he explained. His manner was indifferent which confused me. Usually he was either elated about how much he had won or annoyed at his losses.

"Did you win or lose?" I questioned.

"Oh, I guess I'm ahead by a few bucks," he said as he climbed into bed and turned off the light.

I was still standing in the middle of the room, but an icy wind seemed to suddenly blow around me. He was here now and yet he felt

25

even further away than before. I climbed into bed beside him, and an unfamiliar scent hung in the air. What was happening? Why was I so afraid?

When I awoke in the morning Cliff had already left for work. Scott and Chris were just beginning to wake up. I could hear Scott singing softly to himself. Mentally, I ran through the day ahead. I would make an early appointment with the doctor. The house was still a clutter of toys and decorations from Christmas. Grandma and Grandpa Ananian had only left a few days ago. There was a lot to do today.

Around noon Cliff called to say we'd been invited to a New Year's Eve party. It was short notice. New Year's Eve was tonight. "What should I wear?" I asked.

"Oh, it doesn't matter," he replied and hung up.

"Wait, Cliff!" I wanted to say. "Whose party is it? And—we need to get a babysitter—and Chris still has a bad cold—and the doctor has him on antibiotics and..." but the phone line was dead.

Cliff came home only a short time before we were to leave. He was preoccupied with his own thoughts and irritable with the children and me. I wasn't helping matters any. I just couldn't find anything suitable to wear. My wardrobe was void of fancy evening clothes. Everything I put on made me feel dowdy and unglamorous, not how I wanted to feel tonight. Cliff impatiently pushed me along, "Wear that. That's okay. Come on! We need to leave!"

His manner foretold the evening. That impenetrable wall loomed between us again.

"Cliff, who's giving the party?" I said, trying to make some connection with him.

"Oh, someone from work," he said offhandedly.

"Will there be anyone I know?" I questioned back.

"No, I don't think so. Hurry up!" he barked. "I'm going to wait in the car."

So much for emotional contact, warmth, and a little dialog. I followed him to the car. We rode in silence to the party. I wanted so much for him to touch me, hold me, reassure me that everything was okay. "Cliff, where are you? What is happening between us? I love you. Why am I so afraid?" my unvoiced thoughts shouted.

The party was well under way when we arrived. The house was overflowing with people. Everywhere were couples sipping drinks, laughing, munching, and enjoying the occasion. "Cliff—" I started, but realized he wasn't beside me. I looked around in the sea of faces but Cliff wasn't anywhere to be seen. I wandered aimlessly through the rooms. He had been right. There was no one I knew here—not even one familiar face. I strolled into the kitchen. There was Cliff! He was talking animatedly to a young woman. I came up beside him and put my arm around him in our familiar way. To my bewilderment he took my arm down and stared at me in icy annoyance. He didn't introduce me to the woman. Instead he said, "I'm leaving for a few minutes, Cyndy. Find someone to talk to. I'll be back shortly." He and the girl abruptly left. I stood there, staring into the empty space, until I was bumped from behind by a rowdy couple. I walked back into the living room. Tears were welling in my eyes but I forced them back, squelched them. I sat down on a sofa feeling so terribly alone, so hurt and confused. Where are you, Cliff? Please come back and hold me. Please tell me that I don't need to be afraid.

The party spun and reverberated around me like a meaningless cyclone. Just out of reach were the shards of understanding. My mind was too numb to grab them. I sat motionless as the time sped toward the new decade. People laughed around me but I was oblivious, as in a stupor.

My isolation was breached when a loud voice raucously announced, "Five minutes before midnight! Find your partner for the countdown."

I slowly got up and hesitantly looked for Cliff. The countdown had begun.

"Ten. . . nine. . . eight. . . "

I didn't see him in any of the rooms.

"Seven. . . six. . . five. . . "

I stood in the foyer alone.

"Four. . . three. . . two. . . "

Cliff touched my arm.

"Oh, Cliff," I sobbed in relief. I put my arms around his neck to kiss him.

"Don't do that, Cyndy!" he said roughly as he pushed my arms down. "I have something to tell you." His breath smelled heavily of alcohol. "I'm leaving tomorrow. I'm going to move into an apartment. I need my space. I don't want the responsibilities of a family anymore."

"One. . . "

"Happy New Year!"

CHAPTER 6

I Will Like You Forever

Scottie stood in the foyer of our Texas house looking so very small and vulnerable. The brown wooden beams formed shadows across the floor like an intricate maze. Scott reached for his father. Cliff was holding two suitcases and was impatient to leave.

"Daddy, please don't go," he pleaded. "Why are you leaving?"

"Because I don't love your mommy anymore, Scottie," Cliff said tersely.

"Don't you like Mommy, Daddy?" he asked.

"I like Mommy, Scott, but I don't love her," he attempted to explain.

"I like you, Daddy. Do you like me?" persisted Scott, trying to understand the difference between the two words.

"Yes, Scottie. I like you very much. I love you, son," said Cliff.

"Then don't go! You like us, right, Daddy? You like Mommy. Please don't go!" Scott's voice was getting a little more frantic.

"Son, I do like Mommy but it's not the same as love."

"Yes it is, Daddy. I like you and I love you, Daddy. You said you liked me and loved me. It's the same Daddy! You can stay!" Scott rationalized desperately.

"Scott, I can't. You have to understand. I like Mommy but I don't love her anymore. It's not the same."

"I don't understand," Scott said plaintively. "If you like us why are you leaving? Why are you going, Daddy?"

"You'll understand when you're older," Cliff said as he pried Scott's little hands from his leg. He picked him up for a moment and hugged him.

Scott could not understand and his voice was shrill with frustration. "Daddy, where are you going? I want to go with you!"

"I'm going away, Scott. You be a good boy for your mother, hear? You do as she says and take care of your little brother for me, okay?"

He put Scott down on the floor and walked out the door. Scott called to him, picking the one word his daddy had used that seemed safe, "Daddy, I like you. I always will like you—forever. Will you always like me?"

But Cliff's car had turned the corner and the question stuck in the air, unanswered.

CHAPTER 7

Under God's Wing

Cliff had moved in with the woman from the party; she was a secretary from work. It was all a mistake, I kept telling myself. This isn't really happening. Cliff would never do that! He loves his boys. He always said he loved me. Our marriage had been good—wonderful. We didn't fight or yell at each other. We were always so comfortable together and laughed easily. Ours was not the marriage scenario that leads to divorce. He'll realize what he is doing and come back in a few days, I blindly hoped.

And yet I was left with one persistent question swirling in my head: why? Why had he left? Why? Why?

Sunday morning I was to be confirmed into the Episcopal Church. I had wanted to go to church as a family. The only church Cliff consented to attend was the Episcopal Church. That was close enough. I started attending the Episcopal Church in Richardson. Cliff had gone quite a few times and the boys liked the Sunday school class. But church membership was a bit of a problem. The Episcopal Church recognized Cliff's membership from the Armenian Church but it didn't recognize mine from the Congregational Church—the church of the Pilgrims still rejected by the Anglicans and King Henry VIII. History intruded its pompous and stuffy head. So I had to go to confirmation classes and study church doctrine before applying for membership.

This Sunday was my confirmation day. It was to have been a family affair but I was now sitting in church alone. I irrationally expected Cliff to come back today. I thought, any minute now I'm going to look behind me and see him.

The priest compared confirmation to a wedding and the relationship as one of marriage to the church. As he pontificated, my mind kept challenging God, "What about *my* marriage, Lord? What about my marriage?" My mind was screaming to God when a firm, soothing whisper cut through my cries. "What I have sanctified I will preserve," the internal voice proclaimed. "What I have sanctified I will preserve."

I took this to mean that God had blessed my marriage and he would

31

also keep it together. I hung onto this thought as tightly as a drowning man would a buoy. I was positive God would show Cliff the folly of his course and he would come back—today! *Today* he would return! Desperate minds have desperate expectations.

Cliff did not come back that day... or ever.

That evening I reached the lowest emotional point in my life. I felt not only rejected by Cliff, but rejected by God. I had prayed to Him, fasted, and was sure He would preserve my marriage.

Now I saw that I was nothing more than a silly little child trying to manipulate the Almighty. And I felt He was laughing at me, mocking me in my despair. I was so dejected and distraught I sobbed bitterly to Him. But one profound realization crept into the darkness.

"Even if you are laughing at me, Lord, and mock me, I cannot leave you. I have nowhere else to turn. There is no one else but you. You are my God!"

In the pit of anguish the one core truth of life resonated. God is God. There is no other. I cannot understand His ways but in submission I bow down to His complete omnipotence.

> *Whom have I in heaven but you?*
> *And earth has nothing I desire beside you.*　　Psalm 73:25

Did it really matter when I ignored God's directive to marry a Christian, seven years ago, to marry a person who shared the Lord as Savior and King? I loved Cliff so much; I was sure that was enough. But now my marriage was in shambles and two little boys were left without a father. Was it important? I had tried to tell Cliff about God. But he didn't listen, he didn't see. Temptation came and he had nothing to hold onto. I begged the Lord to bring him back but in the silence I felt God's tears.

Please God, bring him back!

> *If the unbeliever leaves, let him do so... How do you know,*
> *wife, whether you will save your husband?*　　1 Cor. 7:15–16

But God, I had tried to save him. And yet I also knew I had been straddling the fence. "I can't really live for you completely, God, because Cliff wouldn't understand. I'll wait for him to catch up. He'll come to know you and then we can live for you together, okay God?" I compromised.

Now Cliff was gone. On that Sunday night I realized God was everything. There was no room for compromises or fences. It was all or nothing.

But I had so much to learn. My faith and trust in God were smaller than a mustard seed. And the impossibilities of my situation loomed immense. *God, I am so afraid.*

> *"Do not be afraid....*
> *For your Maker is your husband—*
> *the* LORD *Almighty is his name—*
> *the Holy One of Israel is your Redeemer;*
> *he is called the God of all the earth.*
> *The* LORD *will call you back*
> *as if you were a wife deserted and*
> *distressed in spirit—*
> *a wife who married young,*
> *only to be rejected," says your God.*
> *"For a brief moment I abandoned you,*
> *but with deep compassion I will bring you back.*
> *In a surge of anger*
> *I hid my face from you for a moment,*
> *but with everlasting kindness*
> *I will have compassion on you,"*
> *says the* LORD *your Redeemer.*   Isaiah 54:4–8

God...I need your compassion. I am so weak. And my little boys? Who will take care of them, Lord?

> *All your sons will be taught by the* LORD,
> *and great will be your children's peace.*   Isaiah 54:13

I was embarking on a new chapter in my life. Up until now my faith had never really been tested. Life had been good, no struggles, no heartaches. But within a matter of months my world had fallen apart. I found despair to be a deep well with very slippery sides, so easy to fall into but so hard to get back out of. I couldn't balance on the edge alone. I needed God's steadying hand to keep me from falling.

Did it matter when I had not obeyed seven years ago? It mattered, and there are consequences for every action, but even in the despair, God's presence never leaves. He weeps with us, then gives us the strength to go on.

He will cover you with His feathers,
and under his wings you will find refuge;
his faithfulness will be your shield and rampart.   Psalm 91:4

I was under God's wing. He was and is my refuge.

CHAPTER 8
Tangled Webs

It was not long after the divorce, but long enough for three lives to be completely disrupted, then rearranged. His daddy had left, although Scott had pleaded with him to stay. The house in Texas had to be sold and life fell into chaotic disorder. On a very bleak and cold day in February my two small sons and I moved from Texas to my parent's home in northern New Jersey and later, finally, to our own small house at the Jersey shore.

Scott had negotiated the transition in a pensive, quiet manner. He was three when he pleaded with his daddy and now he was a man-child of four. Our new home seemed very threatening to him. Grandpa had confided that he was now "the man of the house." But as he surveyed the shadows forming in the afternoon light, he wanted desperately for someone else to be that man.

In a four-year-old mind, life can secret many ogres and villains in the corners of half-lit rooms. Doors can seem quite flimsy when tasked with restraining these imagined monsters. Always there had been some other man to ward off his fears, to protect him from things that were bigger than he was.

He looked at me carefully. In his eyes I don't think I measured up very well in the house-defending department. I wasn't tall and big like his daddy or grandpoppy. Many monsters surely would be bigger than me. The shadows became deeper and Scott's eyes warily watched for movement in the darker corners. But he said nothing. He just sat quietly, on the lookout.

It was now bedtime, but Scott didn't want to go into his room. This was unusual for him: both Scott and Chris had always been very cooperative at bedtime, for which I was truly thankful.

"Scott, honey, come to bed now. It's getting late," I cajoled.

"Mommy, I can't!" he stubbornly replied, as he continued to sit and watch silently.

"Scott, COME!" I was tired and lacked patience.

"Mommy, if a robber came into our house how would we know?"

"I don't know, Scott. I suppose we would probably hear him. But I don't think anyone would come into this house. It's too small and we have no treasures."

Scott would not be put off easily. "But Mommy, HOW would we know?" he demanded.

I couldn't placate him. He seemed frightened, yet he would not admit it. Suddenly he darted off to the kitchen what-not drawer and returned with a ball of twine and some bells.

Carefully and methodically he began making a web, looping the rope around the door knob, then over a cabinet, across to the other wall, then back again. Interspersed among the latticework of twine he placed the bells. The pattern was intricate. When he finally ran out of twine, he surveyed his workmanship and looked up at me with uncertain eyes. "Do you think we'd hear the robber come in now?" he whispered.

"Yes, Scott, I think we'd hear him now, and I doubt if he could get through the maze you've made."

He seemed convinced and disappeared into his room and into the folds of his blanketed bed.

I thought this web building was only a one-night fancy, and had allowed him to build it to ward off these temporary fears. In the morning I told him to take it down. No one could enter or leave the house through his creative barrier.

But this night also he refused to go to bed until he once again had erected his twine web, bells and all. Each morning it was dismantled but each night he recreated it just as meticulously.

I was becoming both annoyed and alarmed by his nightly insistence on web-building across the front door. Each time I tried to firmly usher him to bed, he would pathetically wail, "Mommy, how'll we know if a bad man comes into our house?"

When in doubt as to what course to take with my children, I have always prayed to the Lord for wisdom. I so seldom seem to have it and He's promised to give it generously. So I prayed as I watched Scott build his web for the umpteenth time: "Oh God, how can I help him fight and conquer the imagined foes he confronts each night? How can I make him feel his world is secure again? Help me, Lord."

I knelt down beside him and cuddled him in my arms. "Scott, the world seems very big and frightening, doesn't it?" His eyes looked wide into mine but he didn't answer. "Scottie," I continued, "if you could see our house as God does, you wouldn't have to be afraid. You would see God's hand lovingly placed over our house to protect us. He knows we are not very big or very strong, but *He* is. He is loads bigger and stronger than any bad man who would ever try to enter our house." Scott's saucer eyes were intent on me but still he didn't say anything. Silently I added "God, show Scott how you truly do watch over us and protect us."

I had not yet persuaded Scott that our house was safe. Nightly the webs continued to be erected.

A week later our neighborhood *was* hit by vandals. The next morning everything looked in order, as I bundled the children into their car seats, except—the glove compartment, which had been jammed for the past three years, was open and all the maps I kept there were scattered on the floor below.

"Hmmm," I muttered. "Looks like we were visited during the night."

"By a bad man?!" Scott erupted.

"Maybe," I mused. "Someone has broken into our car and spent quite a bit of time trying to get into the glove compartment." I surveyed the contents of the car, scanning to see if anything was missing. Scott was like a tension wire, nervously following every move my eyes made. The bad man had actually COME and his trap had not warned him!

The uninstalled CB radio was still there, on the floor. The money I kept on the console was still there. The tape deck was still in place. The glove compartment was now fixed and opening beautifully. The only thing missing were a handful of tapes I kept in the car for the children. Four of them were copies of records I kept in the house. The fifth one was a brand new tape, a Christian tape we had just bought, called "Nathaniel and the Grublets".

Carefully checking, I could find nothing else missing and, even though the boys were upset their tape was gone, I was relieved it was not worse.

I called the police to report the incident anyway, but didn't expect much attention or concern. However, within minutes two squad cars pulled into my driveway. Three officers approached to take the report. With embarrassment, I related that only one children's tape had been taken, and that I only called it in to alert the police to activity in our area.

One of the officers incredulously whistled, "Activity! Lady, you are the forty-second call we've had in this area this morning. And so far you're the only lucky one. Stereo speakers, tape decks, and CB radios have all been ripped out of the cars. Vehicles were vandalized. Anything that could be taken was taken or destroyed in the process. Except your car—you say one tape is all that's missing? Interesting."

The officers finished filling out their report and left. Both boys watched as the squad cars pulled out of the driveway and roared down the street. Scott had not missed one bit of the conversation. His eyes were dinner plates, with fear etching their sides.

I bent down and held him tightly in my arms. "Scottie, do you see what's happened? The big bad man did come but God, who is so much bigger, was watching over our house. He didn't let the bad man take anything except what God wanted him to have. Scottie, do you remember what 'Nathaniel and the Grublets' is about?"

"Yes, Mommy," he quivered. "It's about the little Grublets who decided to steal for a living."

"What stopped them from stealing?" I coaxed.

Scott thought awhile and then spurted out "They met Majesty, Mommy, and Majesty changed their lives. Mommy, the bad man needs Majesty! He needs Jesus!"

"I think God thinks so too, Scott, and that's why that tape was the only thing He allowed him to take. Scott, God's hand is very big. Do you see now how he can protect us even though we, ourselves, are not very big and not very strong? God is the man of our house, honey."

The eyes that looked up at me no longer had fear in them—they were filled instead with a shining realization of the love our heavenly Father has for His children. Scott knew now that God's hand was over our house. No more webs were needed with bells to go ding in the night. There still was no daddy nearby to protect the house, but God had shown Scott that He was ever so much bigger and stronger. *He* was the Man of the house and would watch over always!

> *The angel of the* LORD *encamps around*
> *those who fear him,*
> *and he delivers them.*
>
> Psalm 34:7

CHAPTER 9

A Christmas Wish

So many changes, so many adjustments, in just one year: a smaller house, a smaller paycheck, bigger bills, bigger worries, day care and nursery school, full-time employment, less time at home—Christmas would be just one more adjustment to add to the list.

Last year, another lifetime ago, our house was straight out of *The Night Before Christmas*. A live eight-foot spruce, weighed down with lights and tinsel, sparkled from inside the large bay window of our house. There were so many presents and toys, bows and wrapping, that the tree was almost hidden from view. This year a small green aluminum tree with one strand of lights sat in the corner of the living room. The gifts around the tree were placed with love but could not begin to compete with years past.

There had always been a fireplace to hang the stockings. The boys searched high and low in our little house for a suitable substitute. Nothing came close, not even a niche in the wall. They finally settled on hanging the stockings from doorknobs.

It was hard to find time to shop for Christmas toys. I could not bring the boys with me and I had little money for a babysitter. Checkout lines in the major toy stores had become unmanageably long. Fortunately, one toy store advertised new Christmas hours. They would stay open until midnight! I could handle the cost of a teenage babysitter for one night. But this would require intricate planning to do my entire shopping in five hours.

The day was set. The babysitter hired. I rushed home from a full day of teaching, hugged, fed, and bathed the boys, got them ready for bed, instructed the babysitter, and left numbers for any- and everyone she could call if the unforeseen occurred. Exhausted, I headed out the door for a night of shopping. On the plus side, I discovered there weren't very many other people as harried and short of time as I was: the store was relatively empty from ten to twelve.

Chris was easy to shop for. He was two and wanted whatever was advertised on the television. If it made noise and had wheels he'd be happy. But Scott was more secretive. Every time I asked him what he wanted for Christmas, he would look away, shrug his shoulders, and say "I don't know, Mommy."

"Scott, there must be something you'd like?" I had persisted.

Again he looked away. "It's okay, Mommy. Anything you get me will be okay."

I wanted there to be something under our little tree that would make him happy, make him clap his hands in excitement as he had done last year. But I got no more of an answer as many times as I asked him. I looked about the toy store and felt frustrated that the one special gift couldn't be found.

Christmas Eve, Grandma and Grandpa Ananian invited us to join them for their traditional Christmas Eve party. Cliff wouldn't be attending, since he was in the process of moving from Texas to Alabama with a new wife. But all the other relatives, aunts, uncles, and cousins would be there.

Grandma had decorated the house beautifully. Their tree was exquisite. The house radiated the colors of the season. Great-Grandma had outdone herself preparing the marvelous Armenian pastries. There was a cornucopia of mouth-watering treats and delicacies.

Scott and Chris, being the first grandchildren, had firm hold on the spotlight of the occasion. All of the attention was chaotic and confusing for them. Whispered hints that Santa would come at midnight were repeated in their ears by each relative through the evening. As the night wore on they were so tired, it was an effort to keep them excited and cheerful about anyone's appearance. But somehow, as the clock struck twelve and bells could be heard jingling in the rooms above, the little boys rose to the occasion.

Steve, Cliff's younger brother, was given the honor of the time-worn suit this year. The same faded red pants, the once shiny black belt, and scraggly-looking beard that Cliff had worn last year were now disguising Uncle Steve.

He came down the stairs "HO-HO-HOING" with all the gusto he could muster. The sack swung back and forth on his shoulder as he clumped into the middle of the room. "Merry Christmas, everyone! Ho, ho, ho! Merry Christmas! Have you all been good little boys and girls?" he questioned. He gave a demanding look around the room. "I have lots of toys in my sack for good little boys or girls!"

Last year Chris had wanted no part of this funny looking man but this year—this year was an entirely different matter. The enticement of toys had successfully overcome his wariness. He was curious about the brightly wrapped packages in Santa's bag and was all set to climb up Saint Nick's knee at the first opportunity.

But Scott was the one holding back. He kept staring at Santa, wanting to go to him and yet he hesitated. His eyes searched the face of this newcomer.

"Scott, do you know who that is?" I asked, expecting him to say, "Santa Claus."

"Yes," said Scott, his eyes shining brightly. His whole demeanor was now one of expectancy and joy. "It's Daddy!" he whispered excitedly. "It's Daddy!"

In distress I realized his confusion. Daddy had always played Santa Claus. Scott had recognized him last year. He had hugged him and told him he looked "silly." Tonight Uncle Steve resembled Daddy dressed in this costume.

"No, Scottie. That's not Daddy. It's Uncle Steve, honey," I said gently.

Scott turned away. His little body crumpled. Tears pooled in his eyes. His lower lip trembled. Then giant tears quickly cascaded down his little cheeks. His whole body shook with the tremendous sobs of grief. He loved his daddy. He missed his daddy. He had tried to be so grown up but he was only four. He wanted his daddy to come back and for a brief moment he thought he had. The disappointment was more than he could handle. His sobs silenced the chatter and merriment of the gathering. Everyone stared at the little boy huddled in my arms, inconsolably crying.

"Scott, I thought you were a big boy," chided Grandpa. "You're too old to be afraid of Santa Claus. Look, Santa has a nice, big present for you. Don't you want to see?"

Scott violently shook his head. He buried his face deeper into my chest and wailed. How could I explain to them? I couldn't.

The one gift Scottie wanted for Christmas, Santa would never be able to bring him. He wanted his daddy back.

CHAPTER 10

Your Rules are Too Tough

I knew I needed to find a bible-believing church for the three of us to attend. Fortunately, I found a small Baptist church within a mile of our house. However I discovered I was the ONLY divorced single mom in their midst. As such I received various reactions from those in the church. A few viewed me as a threat, someone to protect their husbands from. A few viewed me as "the woman in sin" and acknowledged that it was a good thing I was attending church but should not be trusted with teaching Sunday School or other church ministries. A few viewed me as a "benevolent project," to reform and save. The majority, however, accepted me at face value and were genuinely friendly.

After I had been attending for a few months, it was announced that a seminar would be held in the Ocean Grove Auditorium. A few well-meaning people decided this was JUST the thing I needed. I did not know who the speaker was and had not heard of his seminars, so I wasn't at all sure I agreed. Plus, the cost to attend was quite high, given my budget, and I would have needed a babysitter for Scott and Chris for the entire week. I KNEW I couldn't afford that.

But the church generously paid for me and I was assured that a woman in the church had volunteered to take care of the boys. I agreed to attend Thursday through Saturday.

On Thursday night I readied the house for the arrival of the babysitter. Everything was tidy and Chris and Scott were bathed and ready for bed. The back doorbell rang, but before I could reach the door, in trudged Mrs. Kulmeyer, pails in both hands, a mop under her arm, and rubber gloves hanging out both pockets! She was a small elderly German woman and had obviously come to do business. I assured her she did not have to exert herself, that once Scott and Chris were in bed she could relax, read, or watch television.

"I hate to be idle, and you, a single mother, always busy with your children. While I am here I might as well be useful, so many things to do in a house," she brusquely answered.

I left knowing my children and my house were in very good hands.

The large Ocean Grove Auditorium was filled to capacity. I had arrived a bit late and found a seat off to the side amid a sea of strangers.

I did not know what the topic for the night would be, but there it was, in big, bold letters across the screen:

—DIVORCE—
SEVEN REASONS WHY YOU SHOULD NOT REMARRY

Wait a minute! I was thirty years old, not particularly ugly, and had no intention of remaining single. The boys needed a father and I wanted a husband. Staying single hadn't even been contemplated.

I sat defensively listening as the speaker expounded his seven reasons. Most of them I didn't feel were substantial enough to pursue a life of singleness.

But one of them concerned the vow I made on my wedding day to God. What had I sworn to Him concerning my husband and the marriage bonds? Was I released from that pledge if my husband committed adultery? The speaker said, "No." I wasn't so sure.

Truthfully, I didn't really know what I had promised God. My marriage ceremony had been performed in Armenian, sung by a cantor as we were doused with oil and bound with golden cord. I hadn't understood a word the priest had said.

I left the Auditorium in a reflective and disturbed mood. The remaining reasons for eternal singleness would be discussed the following night. What I had already heard bothered me enough.

It was late when I returned home. The boys would be asleep and Mrs. Kulmeyer would probably be collapsed in an easy chair, I surmised. As I entered my house the sound of the vacuum cleaner was buzzing away. The kitchen glowed—*radiated*—with cleanliness. Every faucet, drawer handle, glass, and appliance beamed at me. The kitchen floor glistened. The bathroom sparkled. My two pieces of silver shone brighter than Halley's Comet. There wasn't a speck of dust anywhere. And now the living room carpet was being attacked with a vengeance.

I gently tapped Mrs. Kulmeyer on the shoulder to let her know I was home. All I could mutter was, "Wow!" but that hardly seemed sufficient for the transformation my house had undergone. With a very serious face she explained, "Oh, I only did a little. Just a quick clean up job. I don't like to stay idle."

I handed Mrs. Kulmeyer the money for babysitting and she refused to take it. "Oh! No, no, no! You keep that! I don't need any money!" she emphatically stated. Reluctantly Mrs. Kulmeyer relinquished the vacuum cleaner and left, in a clatter of buckets and pails and mops, but promised she'd return the following night to watch my children. I momentarily pondered what there was left in my small house that would keep her from "being idle" one more night. There was absolutely nothing left to clean.

Punctually, she arrived the following night, armed with her cleaning arsenal. I left, not particularly excited about going. I found a seat, again, among hundreds of people I didn't know. I was not one of the happy, acknowledging, receptive faces about me. My face was set in a resentful glare.

Reasons five, six and seven were on the screen. One was based on Matthew 5:32 and Luke 16:18:

> *Anyone who divorces his wife and marries another commits adultery, and the man who marries a divorced woman commits adultery.*

Anyone who married *me* would be committing adultery since I was still bound to my first husband in God's eyes. This reason I didn't like and my resentment flared into anger. I wasn't the one who had committed adultery! My husband had! Why should I be the one punished!

The last reason of the night was the only one that penetrated my defenses. "What statement would remarriage make to my children?" My marriage came to a dead end. If I quickly remarried, would I be saying to my children that marriages are discardable, that the vows taken before God are not to be taken seriously, are not binding, that commitment and sacrifice are not necessary? Would I be saying to them that if you run into trouble, you should take the easy way out, dispose of the marriage, divorce it, and try again? The speaker stressed that staying single was an irrevocable statement to my children that marriage is a lasting decision and commitment before God, to be entered into

ONLY ONCE.

That night I left the auditorium angry. Angry at the speaker and angry at God. In tears I bitterly shouted to God that I loved Him and had wanted to serve Him but if this is what He intended for my life

I could no longer follow. *His rules were just too tough!* I couldn't stay single! I wanted desperately to be loved, valued, and cherished again. I needed a husband and my sons needed a father. I was only thirty years old. The future loomed ominously before me. Forty or fifty years of being alone *terrified* me!

When I returned home all was quiet. My front steps were swept, my back steps were swept, and even my driveway was swept, from street to garage. Mrs. Kulmeyer had done such a thorough job that my neighbors, who had just returned from Florida, thought I had moved out. Who else but a new owner would care how the driveway looked?

The house was immaculate. Mrs. Kulmeyer again, refused to take any money from me. I thanked her profusely for her help but somehow the words seemed totally inadequate to express my appreciation. I did add, though, that she didn't have to return the following night. I wasn't going to be able to go to the last session of the seminar, I lied.

After she left I sat, utterly despondent. I knew I was turning my back on God. God, who had always been with me, had carried me through the emotional devastation of the divorce, had comforted me, sustained me, provided me with a house and a job, had cared for my children, and protected all of us—I was walking away from Him because His rules were too difficult. I was divorced but I had not expected that God would hold restrictions on remarrying.

I stayed away from church. I didn't read my Bible. I couldn't pray. When God entered my thoughts I only cried to Him that His rules were too hard and I couldn't follow anymore. For a month, maybe two, I defiantly avoided God. I was angry and felt betrayed by Him. I didn't want to pray.

One night, however, I awoke to find His presence inexplicably close to me, like a warm blanket on a very cold night. "Child, child," He seemed to be calling.

"Lord, I'm frightened. I don't want to be alone the rest of my life. I want to be loved again," I called back.

"Child, do you love me?" patiently His silent voice seemed to ask.

"Yes, Lord," meekly I whispered.

"Do you trust me?" He whispered back.

"I want to, Lord."

"Do you Trust me enough to know that whether you stay single or whether you remarry, I have chosen what is best for your life?"

My resentment, my loneliness, and my bitter stubbornness melted away. "Yes, Lord, yes." I wept as His love enveloped me.

"Will you follow me knowing that where ever it leads I will always be there for you?" His silent voice echoed in my heart.

Tears drenched my pillow. "Yes, Lord! I'm sorry. Oh Lord, forgive me. I do trust you, God!" I sobbed in joy and relief. The full realization of His love poured over me.

How could I live a life apart from Him? What joy would there be in a union not blessed by my Lord?

The question was not dogmatically answered as to whether I would ever marry again or not. But whether I am single or married it must be by His Will. It is in God's hands to decide and I will trust His choice. What is important is that I am following God in obedience where ever He leads. In submission, I fell into the loving arms of my Lord, whose rules suddenly became very easy.

> *This is what the* LORD *says—*
> *your Redeemer, the Holy One of Israel:*
> *"I am the* LORD *your God,*
>   *who teaches you what is best for you,*
>   *who directs you in the way you should go.*   Isaiah 48:17

CHAPTER 11

The Father's Hand

Grandpa had unearthed two fishing poles in his garage and had given one to Scott and one to Chris. The boys were eager to use them. It was true that we were in the perfect location to take up fishing. Just down the street was an ocean inlet where boys and men were always crabbing among the rocks or fishing off the bridge. Both Belmar and Ocean Grove were nearby and had fishing piers that jutted out into the surf. Avon had jetties. Seeing all this activity it was only natural that the boys would want to learn how to fish. And now they had poles. All that remained was for me to take them.

Scott made me promise early in the summer that I would take them fishing. I had effectively procrastinated for two months but school was going to begin in a few days. The time had come!

"Okay Scott!" I announced at breakfast. "Today is the day! Find your fishing poles, boys. Put on your swim suits. I'll pack lunch."

As the car backed out of the driveway, I could state categorically that I knew nothing about what I was venturing to do. I had never been fishing in my life.

I figured the bait shop around the corner would be a good place to start. With determination I entered the store, both small boys in tow.

"Can I help you?" the weather-beaten angler behind the counter asked.

"Yes," I hesitated. "We're going fishing and I'm not sure what I need."

He scrutinized the three of us and quickly concluded there wasn't a sea-worthy fellow among us. "Well, what are you going for?" he asked.

My blank look told him I hadn't a clue what he was talking about.

"What do you want to catch?" he rephrased.

"Oh, I don't know. What should I be catching?" I naïvely responded.

"Lady, do you want to just *catch* something or do you want to *eat* it too?" He slowly enunciated each word.

"Well, if I'm going to be spending all this time and effort I might as well get something to eat from it in the end!" I retorted.

"Good! Then we'll set you up for snappers," he concluded.

"That will be fine!" I affirmed decisively. I had no idea what snappers were.

The man was gone for a few minutes, then returned with a pail of "swimming things," some yellow and red plastic "ping pong balls," and a few chunks of some kind of metal. "Here. This will do you nicely," he said.

I paid him the money and we were off to—I wasn't sure where! Where would be a good place to fish? Scott volunteered the jetties at Avon. We always saw lots of people fishing there. So to the jetties we went!

The car was parked and we unloaded all our fishing gear: two poles, one bucket full of swimming things, yellow and red plastic ping pong balls, and pieces of heavy metal. As we traipsed across the sand toward the jetties, I confided to the children that we needed to pray.

"Why, Mommy? Is something wrong?" they both chimed.

"Well, not exactly," I confessed. "It's just that we have all these things for fishing and I haven't got the vaguest idea what they're for or what to do with them. We better pray real hard that somebody will help us when we get to the jetties." The boys bowed their heads earnestly and prayed for the needed help.

Help *was* provided. Once on the jetty it didn't take long for it to become obvious that I didn't know the first thing about fishing! An older man with snow-white hair kindly offered assistance.

"The metal things are sinkers and have to be snapped on the line like this. The bright plastic balls are floats and they go higher up on the line, right here. The swimming things are killies. They're used for bait," the man patiently explained.

Then he told me to reach into the bucket and grab one of the killies. This is not a pleasant sensation, but I did manage to grab a slippery little fellow. Then he told me to—stick the hook right through its eye! OH! GROSS! NO WAY! Why couldn't I put it through his tail, at least? The man explained that they often escaped the hook when they were put on tail first. Then he looked over the rocks on the jetty and told me to "cast it out!"

I looked over the rocks on the jetty and thought, "Fat chance!" I tried, gamely, and each time the hook and the poor little killifish went up in the air... and came back down right in front of us. The water had stretched annoyingly out of reach.

Finally, the old man shook his head and said, "Lady, why don't you and your boys go up by the bridge. There you can just let the line drop over the wall and—who knows—you might catch something."

He reached down and took a hand of each boy and carefully guided them over the jetty rocks to the bridge. I thanked him for his help. He was right. It was much easier to just let the lines drop. Scott and Chris both quickly got the hang of that. I relaxed, feeling that—apart from having to put those poor little killies on the hook!—fishing wasn't so bad.

"Mommy! Mommy! I caught something!" Scott's excited voice broke into my reverie.

"Good, Scott! Wow! Pull it in! Let's see what you have!" I encouraged.

Up into the air came a dangling, wiggling snapper more than a foot long. Scott reeled it in and proudly displayed his prize. In his eyes I'm sure it was the size of Jonah's whale. "Mommy, take him off the hook!" he demanded, excited.

I discovered my second reason to not like fishing: there are *teeth* in that fish!

I was holding the line in one hand and the fish's squirming body in the other. As two sets of very sharp teeth rapidly sliced the air, a brilliant thought occurred to me: maybe this is why these fish are called "snappers"!

I was stumped. How was I going to get the hook out of the fish's mouth? I didn't relish having my fingers anywhere near those slashing daggers. I located a twig with the intention of using it to poke the hook out of his mouth. But with one quick chomp the snapper had diced the twig in two. I tried shaking the hook out of his mouth. I shook, and I shook, and I shook, but the hook didn't budge from his jaw. I was about to cut the line with the hook still in his mouth when help arrived once more.

The man from the jetty returned to see how we were making out. Scott and Chris jubilantly showed him our "whale." Without saying a word, the man reached down and deftly removed the hook from the fish's mouth. He congratulated Scott on his fine catch and told him it would make a mighty fine supper that night. With a few more encouraging words, he strolled off on his way home.

With success so recent, both boys wanted to continue fishing. As beginner's luck would have it, they each caught another fish. Chris's was small and I was able to shake it off the hook. But Scott caught another good-sized snapper. It was late in the afternoon and my patience with hooks and piranha teeth had worn out. As Scott swung the fish around, I caught the line and in one even motion, snipped the string. The fish dropped gracefully into the bucket, hook and all.

Scott briefly protested that I had ruined his fishing pole. But I told him it was late and time to go home. The hook could be reattached later.

Back across the sand we trudged: two fishing poles, one bucket, and three snappers. I was all for going to McDonald's but the boys insisted we *had* to have snapper for supper. That was a first—fish over McDonald's!

At last we were home. We unloaded the car and the boys jumped into the shower while I placed the three fish on the kitchen counter.

I was staring at reason number three to not like fishing: I had to clean and debone these treasures. I got out my cookbook hoping it would give me some clue as to how to do this. Any fish I'd ever seen before had already come nicely cleaned, boned, and wrapped in cellophane; occasionally it even had cooking suggestions on the back!

Thankfully I didn't have to search long for my answer. I followed the cookbook's directions and cut off the head and tail, sliced the fellow in half, cleaned out the disgusting stuff inside, and took the bone out, albeit not very neatly. Bless you, Betty Crocker.

The boys thought this was the most wonderful supper they'd ever had. Scott proclaimed on the spot that snapper was his favorite food, even better than pizza and hamburgers.

With shining, eager eyes, both boys asked, "When can we go fishing again, Mommy?"

"Someday, boys. Someday..."

* * *

As I tucked Scott into bed that night, he gave me a big hug and whispered in my ear, "Mommy, when that old man held my hand today— for a moment, just for a moment, I thought God was holding my hand. Do you think He was, Mommy?"

"I'm sure He was, honey. God's son was a fisherman too." I paused for a moment.

52

"Goodnight, Scottie."

And he took the children in his arms, put his hands on them and blessed them.　　　　　　　Mark 10:16

CHAPTER 12

The Cabbage Patch Daddy

The sun fanned through the half-bare trees and scattered its light on the ground below. I watched the children run in and out of its speckled light. Their voices were light and happy, but the chill wind made me shiver. The approach of winter always brought an added feeling of loneliness.

For four years now, I'd been both mother and father to these two little boys, who trustingly looked to me for guidance, protection, security and love. Christopher, who was five now, really didn't know much about fathers. He was only one when his own had left. Now, Daddy was just a man who lived somewhere down south and called every once-in-a-while.

In my zeal I was determined to fill the shoes left empty. I learned to build a tree house, fish for snappers, camp in the Adirondack woods, bat a ball, and make a soap-box racer. All, I hoped, was well. The children were happy and their needs were met.

But one night, after prayers were said and kisses given, Chris reached for my hand and urgently asked, "Mommy, will I grow up to be a mommy or a daddy?"

"Chris!" I incredulously responded, "You will be a daddy, of course! Why would you ask?"

"But Mommy," Chris persisted, "how do you become a daddy?"

"Chris, you're a boy!" I stated rather emphatically. "You will be a daddy. Girls will be mommies."

"Oh," said Chris sleepily.

The light was turned off and Chris quickly fell into a warm, comfortable slumber.

* * *

Christmas was coming and Chris announced he wanted a Cabbage Patch doll.

I quickly responded with a firm, "No!" adding words echoed from my past that, "Boys don't play with dolls."

"Oh," said Christopher.

55

In truth, Cabbage Patch dolls were the current craze and people were waiting months for the chance to buy a doll. The stores couldn't keep them in stock.

Christmas came and went. Only mild disappointment was registered when no doll was found under the tree. After Christmas the tree came down and Chris stood staring in front of the piled tinsel and glitter, gingerly feeling the assorted ornaments. "Mommy?" he queried.

"Yes, Chris?" I responded, as I watched him slowly twirl a tinsel icicle around his small finger.

"Are all daddies bad?"

"No, Chris," I faltered. "Some are good and some are bad, just like all people. There are good ones and bad ones," I attempted to explain.

"But why, Mommy, do the mommies get the kids and the daddies don't when they divorce?"

The depth of that question startled me and I groped for an answer I wasn't sure existed. "Maybe, Chris," I paused and looked at his questioning face. "Maybe some daddies don't know how to take care of children like mommies do. Some might have a real hard time cooking and cleaning and all the other things a home and children need."

"Mommy?" he asked. "Will I know how to do those things?"

"I sure hope so!" I sighed as I thought of his chores he was yet to do that day and a room cluttered with toys. "You can practice right now on your own room," I suggested. Surprisingly I heard him say, "Okay!" as he disappeared into a mound of toys, sheets, and clothes.

Chris was a happy child. As my youngest he did not seem to take life as seriously as his older brother, Scott. Scott was my thinker, my inventor, my worrier and my scholar. Chris liked to play and climb trees, catch a ball, and build a fort. He tried to catch sunshine for a rainy day, and save a flower for "when it's winter, Mommy." Questions about divorces and daddies were not usually a part of his animated dialog.

"Mommy, when am I going to get a Cabbage Patch doll?" Chris inquired at the dinner table a few nights later.

"Oh, Chris! Why do you want one of them? They are so hard to get, and you won't play with it much. It's not like a truck or a bike," I challenged.

"But I want one, a boy. With brown hair and brown eyes, just like me," Chris pleaded.

"No, Chris, I haven't got the money," I stated with finality. That statement, unfortunately, was one often used and had the ring of truth because we seldom did have money for extras. Chris heard this familiar statement and let the topic drop.

It was time for bed and one last story was read before they both scrambled into their bunks. Prayers were said and the light was turned off. As I was leaving the room, I heard Chris's small voice whispering, "Mommy, Mommy."

"Yes, Chris?" I said as I knelt beside his bed.

"Mommy, is Daddy bad?" His face had almost a look of fear and his body was tense as he waited for my answer. Did I have an answer? I was still struggling myself with how I felt about their father. I vacillated between love and anger, resentment and acceptance—but was he bad?

"Honey, when Daddy left it made us feel sad and it hurt very deeply. He was tempted to do something bad and he didn't have Jesus to hold onto. But Daddy isn't bad. He just doesn't know Jesus. He makes mistakes, honey, like many people. Your Daddy loves you, Chris. He's just very far away."

"Oh," sighed Chris. "Mommy, what do daddies do?" he continued.

"Well, I guess they do what they have to do: work, and laugh or cry—and love, especially their little boys."

"Will I know what to do when I'm a daddy?" Chris persisted.

"Yes, honey, you'll do what you do now but in a grown up way." I laughed.

"Oh," he pondered. Then sleepily he added, "I love you, Mommy."

"I love you too, Chris. Good night."

The next day Chris and Scott went to visit Grandmommy. This was always a special treat because she never failed to bring them to a store and let them pick out almost anything they wanted. On this occasion Chris found a kit for making dolls that looked very much like Cabbage Patch dolls. He begged Grandmommy to get it. He was going to make it himself, he announced. Grandmommy was not so sure a five-year-old could handle such a project, but after much pleading, bought it for him anyway. And somewhere on the ride home, Chris extracted a promise from Grandmommy that she would make it for him, with brown hair and brown eyes, just like his.

Chris returned home all excited about the doll Grandmommy was going to make. The day after his visit, he insisted on calling Grandmommy.

"Is my doll finished yet?" he asked excitedly. No, Grandmommy hadn't even started it yet.

The following day Chris, again, begged to call Grandmommy. "Is my doll finished yet?" he questioned imploringly. No, just the pattern had been cut out.

Every day for a week Chris begged to call Grandmommy. Grandmommy was very busy and just hadn't had time yet to make the doll.

On Saturday morning I found Chris in tears. He wouldn't say a word. He didn't ask to call Grandmommy and he didn't want to play with Scott. He just sat on his bed kicking one foot up and down, looking totally dejected. On Sunday his mood had not improved.

On Monday he left for school with his brother and I left for work. Chris's behavior and his desire for a Cabbage Patch doll were on my mind. I couldn't understand why he wanted the doll so badly. How was I going to get one? Would Grandmommy really finish the doll she had started? My concerns overflowed while talking to some friends at lunch. To my amazement, one volunteered that she had an extra Cabbage Patch doll.

An *extra* one! People lined up for hours at the promise of a delivery of ten. Waiting lists in toy stores had names numbering into the hundreds and waiting periods of up to eight months. No one had an *extra* one! Doubting the whole situation, I responded lamely, "That's very nice, but he wants a boy doll with brown eyes and brown hair."

"But this one is a boy, and it does have brown hair and brown eyes!" she laughed back. "And it's yours if you want it."

How she happened to have an extra Cabbage Patch doll with brown hair and brown eyes only God knows—and I thank Him gratefully. The fact remains that Chris was presented with his own Cabbage Patch doll late Thursday night, after Little League practice, supper, homework and his bath.

Solemnly, I read the certificate that proclaimed him to be "daddy" of this fuzzy, brown-haired doll named Stevie Vaughn.[1] Chris sat very still and very seriously as he signed his name to the document promis-

---

[1] You'll find a picture of Stevie on page 113.

ing to care for, and love, this soft, snugly find. When he finished signing it, he took a deep breath and stood up very tall.

Ever so gently, Chris picked up the doll, cradled it in his arms and walked slowly from the room. He looked so small and vulnerable. I wanted to hug him but somehow his manner indicated not now. He had some new purpose that needed to be explored.

The next morning Chris came to breakfast with the doll still cradled in his arms. "Hurry and eat your breakfast, Chris, or we'll be late." That was a standard salutation for weekday mornings.

"But Mommy, I have to take care of Stevie! He needs breakfast and his face needs to be washed, and... Mommy, I already made his bed. Am I taking good care of Stevie?"

"Yes, Chris, but..." The look on his face stopped my curt order to hurry. He looked very intent and concerned. Something was on his mind, something that required more attention than the morning routine would permit. "Chris, honey, you're taking very good care of Stevie. You're being a good daddy to him."

"I am?" His whole face lit up for an instant but then, some uncertainly quickly clouded it again. He ate quietly and every few bites he would offer a spoonful to Stevie.

I hurried the boys along, as it was time to leave. They packed their knapsacks and left to catch the school bus. As Chris ran down the street I caught a glimpse of the doll's foot bobbing up and down from the top of his knapsack. A small chuckle wrapped around my heart.

No further thought of the doll came into my mind until that afternoon, when I arrived at the babysitter's house to pick up the boys. As the babysitter went to get them, I spied Chris in the play room, the doll still cradled in his arms, as he intently soothed a pretended whimper from Stevie. When he saw me, he bounded towards me and his face beamed with an extraordinary discovery that he alone knew.

With all the importance and solemnity a five-year-old could muster, he looked up at me and said, "Mommy, I am going to be a good daddy! *I haven't left Stevie all day, and I won't leave him, Mommy.* I even know how to take care of him. I will be a good daddy!"

With his own declaration of worth and value, he walked confidently out the door to the car, and I finally understood why Chris needed the doll. It was a bridge to a region of mystery and fear that he needed to conquer. A place to meet phantoms of daddies-that-aren't-there, of facing rejection and abandonment; a place to learn that not all daddies are bad and that, yes Chris, one day you will be a very good daddy.

"Mommy?"

"Yes, Chris."

"Stevie says he loves me and that I'm the best daddy in the whole world. I love you, Mommy."

"I love you too, Chris!"

PART II

Honduras: Jungle Mission

CHAPTER 13

Here Am I, Lord. . .
Please Send Someone Else!

Only a few more weeks before school would be out. The trees were in full bloom, the grass already needed to be cut, the world was beginning to slow down for summer. I enjoyed my occupation as a teacher but I loved summers even more. In summer I could be a "full-time mommy."

Tucked away in the corner of our back yard was a green pop-up tent. The tent had taken us camping in the northern Adirondack woods, whitewater rafting on the Delaware River, canoeing in the Jersey Pine Barrens, and cave exploring in the hills of West Virginia. All this gave Scott and Chris the freedom and adventure they longed for and needed. There were woods to explore and games of make-believe to play, lakes to swim and canoes to paddle. I could relax and know my children were happy and safe.

The destination our tent took us three weeks later was to a Christian camp in Central Jersey. The camp provided a daily schedule of activities and speakers. I particularly enjoyed listening to the missionaries. They would tell of life in some far off, untamed part of the world. It sounded so very exotic, and I was always quite content that it was someone else God had called and not me. Even though the hour was early, I enjoyed these talks. I loved looking at the picturesque slides and hearing their incredible stories.

On one particular morning a missionary from Mission Aviation Fellowship was speaking. I found a comfortable seat near the rear of the hall, with my coffee cup in hand to fortify me against the early hour. The lights were turned down and fascinating slides of Honduran jungles appeared on the screen: winding rivers and isolated villages, trees so dense that if a plane accidentally landed among them it would never be seen again; grass huts, dusty roads and wild animals. Astounded by the primitiveness of what I was seeing, I jokingly shared with God, "I *know* you wouldn't want *me* in a place like that!"

The missionary continued on about the many hurdles, mental and physical, that one must leap before going on the field. He talked about the things that must be left behind and placed in God's hands and the commitment one must bring with him. At the conclusion an appeal was made for new missionaries. I *knew* it wasn't aimed at me: after all, I couldn't fly a plane and I'd make a lousy mechanic.

Then there was a question period. The lady directly in front of me had her hand high in the air. She asked, "What is Mission Aviation Fellowship's greatest need?" That was a silly question. Even I knew the answer to that one—pilots or mechanics! Wasn't she listening?

The answer that followed unnerved me. "Teachers," the missionary said. "We desperately need teachers. There are many young families with school age children on the field and we can't get enough teachers. If teachers aren't found, the children must be sent to boarding schools hundreds of miles away, or left behind in the United States with relatives. The families want to stay together but teachers are needed."

I have never felt God's finger so firmly on me as I did that moment. My reaction was not Isaiah's but Jonah's: "No way, Lord! You can't mean me! I have my children to think of, my house, my job, my car payments—and what about my father who's sick with cancer. No way, Lord!"

While I was arguing with God, the auditorium had emptied out. The speaker was walking down the aisle and stopped right by my seat. For some unexplained reason, he was looking directly at me as if waiting for me to say something. Flustered and embarrassed, I stammered, "I'm a teacher. May I have more information concerning your mission organization, please?" He was very kind and enthusiastically jotted down on a yellow slip of paper the name of the man to contact at Mission Aviation Fellowship (MAF) headquarters in Redlands, California.

There was plenty of time to think this over. The summer had just begun. I'd forget all about this in a few days.

The rest of the week we had a marvelous time. We canoed down Cedar River right after a heavy rain storm. The river was swollen and the current was swift, but the challenge only invigorated us. For, as young as they were, the boys could help me maneuver a canoe quite efficiently. Scott was at the front, I was in the rear, and Chris was in the middle, acting as the battering ram whenever we came too close to a bank or a submerged tree trunk.

Twenty canoes began the course with us, but only our canoe and one other made it to the end. In the process we rescued four people whose boat had overturned, and freed a canoe with a VERY large lady in it from a very tight spot. We found her lying flat on the bottom of her canoe, her stomach rising high over the rim like a giant white mountain. The rapid current had wedged her firmly against a low limb that stretched across the stream. She was helplessly trapped. With a few mighty "heave-hos" we sent her floating on her way. We also towed two other canoes that were snagged in the reeds. Chris and Scott felt like heroes.

We returned home at the end of the week with most of the summer still ahead of us. I put the yellow slip of paper from MAF on the kitchen bulletin board. I was *sure* it would get lost there, buried under the predictable mound of accumulated notices, advertisements, cards, and junk. With it, I hoped, would vanish the nagging feeling that God expected me to do something with it.

* * *

It was now the end of August. The boys were dark little berries, scampering across the sun baked sand, darting in and out of the ocean waves. They had made a huge sand castle and decorated it with shells. Chris was looking for crabs by the jetty rocks.

School was just around the corner. Scott would be entering fifth grade and Chris would be in third. In a few days I would have to go back to school to prepare my classroom for opening day. Where had the summer gone?

In the weeks that followed, life picked up its pace. Notices came home from school, activities began again: soccer, piano lessons, Boys' Brigade. Papers started to pile on the bulletin board but that yellow slip never would disappear. It refused to stay buried, emerging at the most inopportune times. With it came a persistent, nagging pressure: God wanted me to do something.

In November I came to the conclusion that I was causing myself unnecessary turmoil. After all, no mission group would accept a divorced woman as a teacher! With this conviction of rejection, I wrote a letter to MAF with a copy of my résumé. It was the most negative job application I have ever written. The résumé contained none of my accomplishments. The letter began with the announcement that I was divorced with two young children:

"I am a teacher but realize that being divorced is not always looked upon favorably by mission organizations. I love the Lord and want to serve him but if being divorced is an obstacle in MAF's eyes, I would *truly* understand."

With such a letter I was sure they would write back and say, "Sorry, all positions are filled," and that would be the end of the matter.

Instead, a few nights later I received a long-distance telephone call from MAF in California. The voice apologetically asked what the circumstances of my divorce were. After his questions were answered, my divorce was deemed a "Biblical divorce."

I wasn't sure if that was good or bad.

A week later a letter arrived from MAF saying they definitely did need teachers and they already had a place for me in a school in Guatemala, Central America.

I did not jump for joy.

The Lord and I began a long series of "discussions": "Lord, I have enough to do taking care of Scott and Chris. What about my job? I can't risk that security, Lord. And my car payments—how will I be able to meet them? My house, Lord! I have mortgage payments to make as well! And have you forgotten that my father is sick? What if something were to happen to him and I was far away, Lord?" But despite all my perfectly good excuses I did not feel a release from God's gentle pressure and His persistent call.

During my devotion on one very anxious day, my eyes fell on Luke 14, the Parable of the Great Banquet:

> *Jesus replied: "A certain man was preparing a great banquet and invited many guests. At the time of the banquet he sent his servant to tell those who had been invited, 'Come, for everything is now ready.'*
>
> *But they all alike began to make excuses. The first said, 'I have just bought a field, and I must go and see it. Please excuse me.'*
>
> *Another said, 'I have just bought five yoke of oxen, and I'm on my way to try them out. Please excuse me.'*
>
> *Still another said, 'I just got married, so I can't come.'*
>
> *The servant came back and reported this to his master. Then the owner of the house became angry...*

*'I tell you, not one of those who were invited will get a
taste of my banquet.' "*

A conviction fell on me: did my excuses all have parallels in this
story? "Lord, is the field and my house in the same category?" I
silently asked. "And would my car be a modern day version of an
ox, Lord? Would the third man's marriage excuse fall into the same
category as my responsibilities to my children and sick father?"

For so long I had been praying, "Use me, Lord," and now when
he wanted to use me, all I could give Him were excuses. The Banquet
was before me but I was afraid to go in. "Lord, I'm frightened," I
prayed. "How do I enter your Banquet? How can I be sure this is your
will for me?"

His gentle answer was, "Enter one step at a time. The doors will
open to reveal my path."

With God's help I timidly followed, one step at a time, still secretly
hoping some door would close—soon!

I met with my pastor and deacons to discuss my intentions and my
fears. I continued my correspondence with MAF, but in the meantime
they had changed my placement from a major city in Guatemala to one
of the most primitive settlements in Central America: Ahuas, Honduras. This was a tiny and remote Indian village in the jungles of the
Mosquito Coast, only 50 miles from Nicaragua—a country frequently
in the news with civil unrest and fighting between the *Contras* and the
Sandinistas. It was the very place I had seen in the missionary's slides
the previous summer.

When I was informed of my new placement, my minor apprehen-
sions broke out into major panic. "Lord!" I cried. "They're fighting
down there! My children and I could get killed! It's a jungle there—
a *real* jungle with snakes and alligators, bugs and parasites and heat.
Lord, we could disappear and no one would ever know. Lord! I can't
go to a jungle, right next door to the Contras and Sandinistas!" My
prayers were tense pleas to God, but I couldn't lose the conviction that
He wanted me to serve Him in this remote jungle village.

The prospect of being near war and fighting paralyzed me. I could
not move forward, but I couldn't turn my back on God, either. In the
middle of my anguish, God spoke to me:

Tyranny will be far from you;

67

you will have nothing to fear.
Terror will be far removed;
*   it will not come near you....*
See, it is I who created the blacksmith
*   who fans the coals into flame*
*   and forges a weapon fit for its work.*
And it is I who have created the destroyer to work havoc;
*   no weapon forged against you will prevail,*
*   and you will refute every tongue that accuses you.*
This is the heritage of the servants of the LORD.   Isaiah 54:14–17

God was once again assuring me that he would protect us, but my trust was being severely tested. Could I leave my job, rent my house to who-knows-who, trust Him with the well being of my children, leave my comfortable life, and follow Him to a complete unknown?

Before I could leave the country I needed the children's father to give his consent. This could be the door that would close, I hoped. Why hadn't I thought of this earlier? No way would he allow his children out of the country. I intended to make the call as bleak as possible.

"Hello. I called to discuss with you a move the boys and I might make for a year. I was thinking about being a missionary in the jungles of Honduras, about 50 miles away from Nicaragua—you know, where all that fighting is taking place. Would you have any objection?"

His answer totally confounded me. "No, go ahead. It sounds like it would be a great experience for the boys."

Didn't he hear what I said? In disbelief I mumbled, "Great," and hung up the phone.

The next step I needed to take was to get a year's leave of absence from my school district. Here, also, a door could close and I would be off the hook. I met with my principal and wrote a letter to the board with my request for a leave of absence and my intention of serving as a missionary in Honduras. I was sure they were going to fire me on the spot for insanity!

Instead, my leave was granted and I was given permission to take all the books I needed from the used-book storage room. I had recently learned from MAF that I would be teaching ten students in a one-room schoolhouse spanning kindergarten through sixth grade. All my books for every subject were now provided from a secular public school!

In spite of the fact that every door was swinging wide open with every step I took, I was still terrified and anxious. Nightly I had what I called my "Jungle Dreams," imagining myself stranded and lost in a distant land with no way of returning. I met with my pastor once more, intending to tell him I didn't think I could really go through with this.

His counsel was wise. He never told me to go or not to go. That was between God and myself. But he did say that no decision should be made on the basis of fear. He quoted 2 Timothy 1:7:

> *For God has not given us the spirit of fear, but of power, and of love, and a sound mind.*

The fear was not from God.

That night I humbly knelt down and gave God my fear. As I laid it before Him a tremendous sense of relief and joy flooded over me. The panic and anxiety lifted.

For the first time I didn't give God a list of all the things I needed. I submissively asked Him, "What do you need, Lord?"

His quiet answer was, "A teacher—for ten children in an isolated jungle village in Honduras."

With a peace only God can give I responded, "Here am I, Lord. Send me."

> *See, I am sending an angel ahead of you to guard you along the way and to bring you to the place I have pre-pared.*   Exodus 23:20

CHAPTER 14

Grandpoppy

"Lord, take care of my Father while I'm in Honduras. Please watch over him and keep him safe."

My father was 80 years old. A malignant tumor had been discovered between his heart and backbone. Its location made it impossible to operate. The doctors were carefully watching and waiting. I couldn't bear the thought of something happening to him while I was thousands of miles away.

Memories swirled around me. I remembered the long and difficult journey down the aisle on my wedding day. Difficult for him because I was the youngest, the last to leave his nest. In the foyer of the church, just as the wedding march began, my father cleared his throat, held onto my hand and begin to speak.

"Cyndy, girl, I just want you to know you have given your mother and I..." Tears welled in his eyes. He fought for composure as we began our trip down the aisle. Once more he tried.

"Cyndy, girl, you have given your mother and I twenty-two wonderful..." The tears welled up again. He stoically looked ahead, coughing to check the giant lump forming in his throat. We were down at the altar now. He was to let go of my hand and present me to my husband-to-be.

"Cyndy, girl," he whispered. "You have given your mother and I twenty-two proud and..." The last words were barely audible as his voice faltered. He never did finish, his words caught in an eddy of emotion. He refused to allow the tears to have their course, but his eyes glistened as he held my hand tightly, then placed it into the hand of my young husband.

I remember his joy when my sons were born, especially Chris, whose newborn face had the wizened old look of Grandpoppy without his glasses on. A special bond formed between them that first day in the hospital.

When my marriage fell into a million pieces, my father was there and, if he could, would have collected each tiny fragment and patched them together on the sheer force of his love.

When we returned to New Jersey, it was to my parent's home. Dad had every expectation that we would remain with him indefinitely. His child had come home and he was ready to shelter and support my little family.

He had difficulty understanding my desire to start a life of my own. But he had provided me with a college education, a means of support, and the time had come for me to use that profession.

When I bought my small house he was not at all sure it was wise. The investment was good but he worried about my living alone with no man in the house to protect me. Once I had moved in, he was there regularly, "checking the house for needed repairs," he said.

My father's features and mannerisms were reflected in my son Chris's face. Grandpoppy dearly loved both my sons but especially Chris. Grandpoppy was a tease. Scott, at times, was intimidated by this but Chris thrived on it. He would play along with the game right to the end, and if he could, he would turn the tables around on Grandpoppy. They shared a zany wit that found humor in the most ordinary places. Grandpoppy was there to cheer Chris on, in soccer or little league, piano recitals and school plays. Chris had needed Grandpoppy to stabilize his world.

My father was not a religious man. Dad had taken God at His word that Sunday was a "day of rest" and spent the day stretched out on the chaise lounge, enjoying the peace and quiet. My first summer back in New Jersey, I wanted to take the boys camping. Our destination was "Word of Life," a Christian camp in upper-state New York. Dad was not in favor of this venture. He felt it was too dangerous for a single woman to be camping in the woods with two small boys. I attempted to explain to him that we would be in a secure camp area, not in the untamed wilds of the Yukon.

When he realized he could not dissuade me from going, he did an about-face and decided he and my mother would go camping also. He was going to protect me one way or the other.

"Dad," I warned, "It's a Christian camp. You'd be expected to go to all the meetings and lectures. Think of it, Dad, it would be like going to church every single day of the week, three times a day!" He gamely agreed to the terms and we were off to "Word of Life."

Dad stuck to his part of the bargain and did not miss one of the meetings. But when they were over he was always the first to return to our camp site. I enjoyed having Mom and Dad with us. Mom and I shared the cooking and Dad took long walks with Scott and Chris. Silently I prayed for my Dad's salvation.

On Wednesday it was my turn to prepare lunch. The morning session was over. Scott and Chris were bubbling about a trip they and the other children had taken that morning to the Word of Life Ranch.

"Mommy, we saw horses and sheep," exclaimed little Chris.

"There was a real sheriff with a silver badge," added Scott.

"He had a gun!" Chris piped in.

"And there were bandits, too," Scott enthusiastically related.

Chris did not share Scott's enthusiasm about the bandits. "They scared me, Mommy."

Lunch was ready but my Father was nowhere around. I left the sandwiches and soup on the table for Mom and the boys to eat and went to locate Dad. He wasn't in the camp store, or by the pool; he wasn't visiting any of our neighbors or at the camp office. The last place I looked was in the little chapel where the meetings were held. The place had emptied out an hour ago and all was quiet as I opened the screen door. One lone figure was sitting half way up the aisle. His head was bowed, his shoulders were faintly trembling. I walked up to my dad and laid my hand on his shoulder. He looked up and tears were on his cheeks.

Intuitively I understood. "Daddy, did you just meet Jesus?" I whispered.

With radiant but tear-filled eyes he slowly nodded his head. He tried to speak but the words wouldn't come. He just held my hand and smiled, a beautiful glorious smile.

That was seven years ago, and Mom and Dad had been faithfully attending church and growing in the Lord from that day on. Now I was putting my father into God's hands, asking him to care for him and keep him safe while I was away.

The phone abruptly rang. It was late at night. The voice on the line was my sister.

"Daddy has just been rushed to Pascack Valley Hospital. He's in critical condition, Cyndy. He might be dying. Can you come right now? We'll meet you at the hospital. Mommy's already there."

I woke Scott and Chris, grabbed their clothes and rushed to the car. I drove the hour and thirty minutes with the speedometer pushed way past the limit. In the waiting room I found Mom, my sister, her husband and six of their eight children. My brother had been called and was on his way from Tennessee. His plane would arrive in a few hours.

Dad's tumor had metastasized. He was on a respirator. The doctor gave my mother a grim prognosis.

We huddled about, each sending urgent prayers to God for Dad. Scott and Chris were curled up asleep on the waiting room couches. We anxiously waited for the doctor to let us in to see Dad.

Six in the morning, Dad had stabilized enough for us to see him. I was the last to go into his room; I didn't want to see the victory cancer had cruelly taken on my strong and loving father. His white form lay motionless, surrounded by wires and tubes. The respirator wheezed beside him and a tube was placed down his throat. He couldn't speak. A pad of paper was on the table beside him.

As I came to his bedside I reached for his hand—the strong hand that had held mine so many times before, the hand that had given mine away on my wedding day, the hand that steadied me through each crisis. How would I be able to continue on without this hand to reach for when storms seemed black and engulfing?

Tears were in the corners of his eyes. "Poppy, are you in pain?"

He shook his head, no.

"Are you uncomfortable? Can I get you something?" I smoothed his white hair off his forehead.

Again he shook his head, no.

"Poppy, are you afraid?"

His tear filled eyes looked directly into mine as he slowly nodded, yes. Dad had given his life to Jesus but he was now at the critical brink, where words of faith become a reality. What would he find in the shadows of death? Would his Lord really be there? The unknown had daunted him and he stumbled.

"Jesus," I prayed, "hold his hand. Hold his hand, the hand that had held mine when I was frightened. Comfort him, Jesus. Guide him where he must go."

I read 2 Timothy 4:6 from the Bible I had found in his room:

> *And the time has come for my departure. I have fought the good fight, I have finished the race, I have kept the faith. Now there is in store for me the crown of righteousness, which the Lord, the righteous Judge, will award to me...*

Daddy's tears were streaming down his pale cheeks.

> *Even though I walk*
> *through the valley of the shadow of death,*
> *I will fear no evil,*
> *for you are with me;*
> *your rod and your staff,*
> *they comfort me...*   Psalm 23

Jesus was surely holding my Father's hand. The fear had left his face. His eyes were radiant. He couldn't say a word, but he smiled, the same beautiful glorious smile he wore when he first met Jesus.

His vital signs plunged upward. His whole countenance reflected peace.

My brother had arrived and, en masse, the whole family entered Dad's room and surrounded his bed. The twinkle was back in his eyes. He reached for little Chris's hand and squeezed it. On the notepad Dad wrote,

"Thank you for coming to my going-away party."

His ever-present humor had not diminished.

That night, June 7, 1987, with his hand firmly clasped in the hand of his Lord, Dad went to receive his crown. God brought him into His perfect care.

> *... Surely goodness and love will follow me*
> *all the days of my life,*
> *and I will dwell in the house of the LORD*
> *forever.*

CHAPTER 15

Hurdles

"Even before a missionary takes his or her first step in the land to which God has sent him, the most difficult hurdles have already been scaled." These were the words the missionary speaker had said at Keswick Campgrounds almost a year before. At the time I could only vaguely guess at the nature of those hurdles. Now I knew exactly what those hurdles looked like, felt, meant, and required. The whole foundation of my self-sufficient security had been picked up, shaken, and spun around. My job and means of supporting myself and my children were now on hold, future status: unknown. My house was packed up, stored into a multitude of boxes in the attic. Strangers were going to be moving into *my* house, using *my* furniture—*live* in my house! What condition would my house be in when I returned in a year? The boys were leaving opportunities that only the United States could give them, to live in a jungle without modern medicines. What if they got sick? What if they hated the place and wanted to come home? Could we? My father had only recently passed away and I hated leaving my mom alone. I was now going to have to depend on people I barely knew to support me, to send money on a regular basis for my most rudimentary requirements of life. Mortgage payments and car payments still needed to be made even if I was out of the country. Would I have enough to do this? Would my children's schooling be adequate?

A thousand things had to be done before I left. After renting my house and packing up its contents, I had to get a will made, get typhoid and hepatitis shots, get tickets, passports and visas, and a notarized letter from Cliff for permission to take the boys out of the country. I had to learn to cut hair, study Spanish, find a place for my car, make repairs around the house, clean out drawers and closets, open a joint checking account with my sister, obtain books and send them, have a forwarding address for my utility bills, buy additional supplies and clothes, and finally, raise adequate support. Did I have the energy to do all this?

Hurdles! Hurdles! I knew what they looked like. Etched all around them, hanging onto each rung was insidious *Fear*. When I tried to jump the hurdles on my own strength, I fell back, quaking and afraid. The strength to leap into the unknown comes only from God. *Trust* is the opposite of fear, and the pole that can launch us over the most daunting of hurdles. But I was having difficulty hanging onto that pole. I had to trust Him with my job, with my children, with my house, with my finances, and with my very life. These were the truths I had to wrestle with in the months before we left. These were the hurdles that caught my heel as I tried to leap.

CHAPTER 16

Welcome to Ahuas

The day of departure finally arrived: August 25, 1987. The flight to Honduras would leave at 8:10 A.M. from Newark Airport. The airline was called CHALLENGE Airlines, a rather definitive statement to the whole venture. "I, a single mom with two young boys, was going to live in a *very* remote area of Honduras for one year," I marveled. That word "remote" had been worrying me for months. On the other hand, Scott and Chris were completely enthralled by the prospect. I had tried to paint for them as dismal a picture as possible,[1] so they would be prepared for the "remote." But "dismal" and "remote" did not have the same effect on them as it did on me. Their spirits weren't dampened one iota.

We arrived in Tegucigalpa, the capital of Honduras, at 4 P.M. The airport was a postage stamp, nestled between two "Goliath" mountains, with a skimpy runway in the middle. This made for a memorable landing! As soon as the plane touched ground, all brakes were applied full force. I, as well as everyone behind me, found my nose firmly planted in the seat in front for the duration of the landing, which I hoped would end before contact was made with the first mountain!

We disembarked into the heat of the tropics. People were everywhere: behind windows, behind fences, sitting on roofs, even in trees. The attraction appeared to be the landing of our plane. "Maybe more planes didn't manage to stop in time than I wanted to know about," I conjectured. Whatever: we had arrived.

We were met inside the terminal by Roy, one of the missionaries from Mission Aviation Fellowship. He and his wife, Sue, would be our host family until we left for Ahuas in five days.[2] Ahuas! The subject of so many of my frightening "jungle" dreams, the Indian village nestled beside the Patuca River on the northern edge of Honduras, known as the *Mosquito* Coast! Could a name be any more descriptive?

---

[1] Ed. note: in particular, by feeding us nothing but frozen Mexican food from the supermarket for a month, "to prepare us." We'll see what we really ate in chapter 17!

[2] A photo taken in the home of Roy and Sue is on page 113.

"The village has the only medical clinic for a hundred mile radius," Roy explained. "It's run by the Moravian Church and the planes bring the sick to the hospital. There are two missionary pilots and two missionary doctors stationed there, as well as staff from World Relief who work with Nicaraguan refugees."

"Oh," was all I could respond.

Five days later the small MAF Cessna took off. We traveled two hours over barren land, jungles, and marsh. On the last stretch we followed the winding, ox-bowed Patuca River until the pilot pointed below us and said, "There's Ahuas!" From the air it looked like one giant swamp with a few murky tea bags floating in the center. As we drew closer little thatch-roofed huts appeared with one muddy road cutting through the middle. On the periphery of the village were the missionary homes, the school, a Honduran army outpost, and the dirt landing strip which we were headed for.[3]

With a THUD and a SPLAT we landed—right into the wet, mucky mire! Mud was everywhere. This was *not paradise!* Only the boys embarked eagerly. They took off running—no, more like slipping and sliding—ahead to inspect the little hut we would be living in for one year. I cautiously followed.

The little hut was up on stilts, about eight feet off the ground. There was a breezeway between the house-part and the school-part. The school was just one room with primitive, wooden desks haphazardly placed about. Faded art work hung precariously on the walls. This is where I would be teaching ten missionary children. I gulped.

The house-part was divided into one bedroom and one living area. The bedroom was so tiny it looked like a left-over prop from Munchkin land. Someone had built a crude bunk bed for the boys. My cot was ten inches away from theirs and that was the whole width of the room.[4] A tiny closet was against the other wall and that was it. Oh yes, there was a bathroom, not an outhouse. In truth it was an elevated outhouse with a real toilet placed over a pipe that went into a hole in the ground. But I didn't have to go outside, and it had a door. This was a good thing!

The living area had a kitchen with a refrigerator powered by a kerosene flame (which kept blowing out, I later discovered), a stove

---

[3] Aerial photo on page 114.

[4] See for yourself on page 115.

powered by a butane tank under the house, and a sink with indoor water. This was real luxury for Ahuas. There also was a hard, plastic, seaweed-green sofa and a matching side chair with legs partially termite-eaten. Continuous windows encircled the structure to catch breezes in the tropical heat. There were screens on the windows (another luxury) but the screens were skewed every which way. (A few hours later I would realize how serious an issue these "skewed" screens were!) Tattered, floral curtains drooped at sporadic intervals along the windows. The wood walls were shellacked and dark. The humidity had made the veneer coating buckle and wrinkle like and old woman's skin. The sweet-sour smell of mildew and sweat permeated every nook and cranny.

Hanging over the one table in the kitchen was a stark, bare light bulb. A second light bulb hung in the ceiling in the bedroom. The only time these worked, though, were between the hours of 7 and 9 at night when a small generator supplied electricity to the clinic and the four missionary homes.

The inspection of the house was completed. It was no Taj Mahal but it would do I determinedly resolved. We had no food yet so another missionary family had invited us to have supper with them our first night. Evening was quickly approaching. I quickly learned "tropic days" are much shorter than what I was used to. Long shadows stretched across the marshy terrain. I looked out at the muddy path we would have to follow and realized there wouldn't be any street lights to guide us back at night. I then had the brilliant idea of turning on the switch to both of our electric lights and leave them burning so we could see our way back later! I was a GENIUS!

We set off for dinner. The family next door was a wonderfully friendly couple. They were young, in love, and the new parents of four-month-old Jesse. Steve was a pilot and Debbie had her hands full caring for a baby without any of the modern conveniences. We ate spaghetti and sauce for supper and didn't leave to come "home" until about 8:30.

Yes, the two lights were still burning in the little house. We easily followed the beacon along the slippery path, up the steps and into the house and—EGAD!

All I could do was stare in utter revulsion. The whole house was alive! The floor moved in a continuous wave of tiny black ants. Each light bulb was completely encased in an orb of flying gnats, mosquitoes, and other various buzzing things. The sink was layered five and six deep with beetles and roaches. ROACHES! Roaches three and four inches long were playing tag up and down the counter and shelves—hundreds of them, maybe millions as far as my panicking mind was concerned. Dead bugs lay scattered in a black veil on the table under the light. Chris, standing beside me, exhaled and I heard him hoarsely whisper, "Gross!" I couldn't agree with him more. We weren't the only ones that had found our house by the beacon of light. Still crawling in from around the skewed screens were a hundred more beetles and gnats and mosquitoes and other flying things. There is a rock solid reason why this area is called the MOSQUITO Coast.

The bedroom offered another wonderful trove of discoveries. The light between the beds had invited all the bugs in *La Mosquitia* (who weren't already in the kitchen) to spend the night on our nice hard mattresses. Things were buzzing and crawling everywhere. I hadn't put up the mosquito netting yet. I didn't even know *how* to put up the netting and my watch said there was only thirty minutes more of electricity. I rigged netting as best as I could around the lower part of the bunk. Scott and Chris would be secure there. But my bed was more of a problem. There was nothing to string the netting from. The buzzing insects were nerve-racking. And suddenly—I was plunged into total darkness. It was nine o'clock. My bed was still wide open to attack. Helplessly I wrapped the netting around myself and curled up in complete misery.

Then Act Two began. As soon as the lights went out, the walls and ceiling came alive with chirps and squeaks and scratchings and growls! The bugs owned the downstairs of the house but the *bats* owned the attic. And their act was on now! All night long I could hear things moving around in the dark, scratching and growling, only a few inches from my head. Were they inside the wall or out? In the dark I couldn't tell. But wherever they were, they wore combat boots. Growling, hissing, buzzing, biting, scratching. Things were moving in and out of the netting I had wrapped around myself. All night long I kept praying to God to keep me from despair and panic. This was only day ONE!

Morning did arrive, about a millennium later. All the millions of bugs magically disappeared into hidden holes and crannies, to wait again, malevolent, for the next night. The bats took off their combat boots and resumed a quiet siesta.

Scott and Chris woke up refreshed and eager to commence this new adventure. I didn't wake up since I never fell asleep in the first place. But I did get up.

I was covered with bug bites: my arms, my face, my legs. But I was resolved to realign every screen properly, all thirty of them, tape up any additional openings and procure more mosquito netting before another nightfall. I would not let the invaders catch me unprepared again—if only I knew where to get twenty cans of bug spray in the jungle.

As the second night began, there were considerably less bugs, although the bats were just as noisy. An especially loud group were doing gymnastics right above my head. I snuggled under the mosquito netting and hoped that this night I would be able to sleep.

Two in the morning I awoke with intense stomach cramps! For the rest of the night the bathroom and I were extremely close friends. Having no electricity, and no candles yet, I groped blindly in the dark. I found it very disconcerting to be in a pitch-black bathroom with squeaks and chirps all around me and not know who I was sharing the room with. By morning I was spent, only to have Chris and Scott awake with stomach cramps also. All of us were battling for the bathroom! In the peak of intense need the toilet gave out. It just wouldn't flush. With a plaintive gurgle it surrendered, with a white strand of toilet paper waving in submission. I was so sick I could barely move. An Indian workman walked by our window and I called to him that our toilet didn't work any more and we *needed* it. He nodded in consent. About fifteen minutes later I had to make one more urgent dash to the bathroom. I opened the door and found a huge hole in the floor but *no toilet.* I looked over the railing and saw the workman walking away with the commode over his shoulder.

"Hey!" I hollered. "What are you doing with our toilet?"

He shrugged and replied, "You said it didn't work anymore, so if it's broken you don't need it. I'm taking it away."

"No, you don't understand," I lamely tried to explain. "Without it I just have a gaping hole up here. I didn't want you to take it away. I just wanted it fixed!"

He shook his head from side to side and came back up the stairs with the toilet. He reattached it to the floor and left. It still didn't work but I wasn't going to utter a word! Who knew what they'd take away next?

In the late afternoon Chris had a fever. The temperature outside registered almost 97 degrees but he was in his bed shivering. He wanted a blanket and I couldn't even find one. He said he was cold so I wrapped towels around him. A restless sleep over took him but an hour later he awoke screaming from a bad nightmare. I held him in my arms and gently rocked him back and forth. "God, please help," I wept.

We'd only been in Ahuas three days and so far we'd been mired in mud, attacked by bugs, invaded by bats, taken over by roaches. We were sick as dogs. We had no food, because the refrigerator didn't work (no kerosene). The stove didn't work (no butane). The toilet didn't work (no flush). And it had been raining torrents since we'd arrived. We still had ten more months of life in Ahuas to look forward to.

"I can't do this, Lord," I wept again. "I can't do this," I repeated as I fell asleep still holding onto Chris.

When we awoke on the fourth day the sun was shining gloriously. We all felt wonderful. Butane for the stove and kerosene for the refrigerator were obtained. In the afternoon a plane arrived from Tegucigalpa with our suitcases, supplies, candles, flashlights, and boxes of food. And best of all, sitting on the top of one of the boxes, were *twenty cans of bug spray!*

Praise God! I think we're going to make it.

"Dear Lord, Protect us from things that go bump in the night, and also buzz and squiggle and zing! Amen!"

I can do everything through him who gives me strength.

Philippians 4:13

CHAPTER 17

Pass the Pepper, Please!

Shortly after we arrived in Honduras—while still in Tegucigalpa, the capital—I learned that food purchasing would take on a whole new significance. Sue, our hostess, took me to a local supermarket to buy groceries for our trip to Ahuas. I was amazed to see how large the store was. Aisle after aisle was stocked with American brands of food. Familiar packages, with their English labels still on them, were everywhere. It was just like walking into Foodtown back home. This was okay!

I started down the aisles, confidently filling my cart, as I usually did in my weekly shopping.

"Are you sure that'll be enough?" Sue inquired as I put one Uncle Ben's package of rice in my cart.

"What do you mean? One package of rice is always enough for the three of us." I said defensively.

"Yes—but will it last for two months?" Sue continued.

"Two months! Why should it have to last two months?" I skeptically replied.

"You have only one chicken in your basket," she noticed. "And those fresh vegetables—they won't stay fresh for two months."

I didn't like how she kept repeating those words *two months*. "Why do I have to get enough for two months?" I asked again.

Sue gave me a sympathetic look and sighed. "There will be no supermarkets in Ahuas," she patiently explained. "You won't be able to depend on flights from Tegucigalpa to bring in your food regularly. So you'll have to stock up on enough food to last you for awhile, probably two months, until another flight comes into Ahuas."

I was speechless! Shop for two months of food! I didn't know where to begin. What would I need? How much would the three of us eat in two months?

"Also," Sue resumed, empathetic to my total ignorance, "The few items you already have will cost about two hundred dollars when you check out."

She picked up one box of Cheerios nestled in my cart and explained the dollar equivalent to lempiras for that box. THAT box alone would cost me ten dollars! Ten dollars for a small box of Cheerios! The rest of the prices were equally exorbitant. American brands were familiar but VERY, VERY expensive. I unloaded my cart and began all over again. What would I need?

Sue tried to help. She told me I wouldn't be able to use store bought bread. I would have to bake all my own, as well as cookies, rolls, and desserts. I had never baked a loaf of bread in my life! She suggested starting off with forty pounds of flour, local brown sugar in clear plastic bags, buckets of shortening, yeast, and salt. We then added bags of rice, sacks of beans, and numerous cans of vegetables. Milk, I discovered, didn't come in the dairy section but in a very large container filled with dry, white powder. Four or five of these large cans would last us—I hoped. Forget American cereals. Local oats would have to do. Sue also explained that some things like beans, eggs, fruits, and some vegetables could be bought in Ahuas in a pinch.

I did buy ten whole chickens and twenty pounds of chopped beef. These were the "iffy" items. Sue warned me that refrigeration wasn't a dependable commodity in Ahuas. There was a large chest freezer, powered by kerosene, that the missionary families shared in the village, but the kerosene flame had a tendency to go out, and the food would spoil before the problem was discovered.

I found shopping for long intervals of time to be one of the hardest things to do. I never did seem to get it just right. I would run out of an essential staple weeks before the next flight was expected. A five pound bag of flour that would have lasted me months in the States would be gone in just a few days. Sugar and lard all but vanished.

So within the first few weeks in Ahuas, I learned that I had NOT shopped well, the freezer flame DID go out, and all the meat I bought HAD thawed and spoiled.

The one highlight was that the *quince de septiembre* was approaching. This was the Honduran Independence Day, celebrated on September 15. A parade and village picnic were planned and all the Miskito Indians came out in their finest. Two grade school children were nominated as King and Queen for a day.

And! *A COW WAS KILLED!* The meat would be sold for only twenty cents a pound to anyone who wanted it. I was really excited about this! In my mind I was already picturing a ribeye steak, a bit of sirloin, and maybe even a little rump roast. Our diet had been short of meat for a few weeks now.

I was told that if I did want to buy meat I would have to be in the field, by the village church, as close to five in the morning as possible.

"Why?" I naïvely asked.

"Because," it was explained, "the cow is killed at sunrise and lays in the field from then on. Unless you don't care how long it sits out in the hot sun, with bugs and dogs all over it, it's best to get the meat as close to the kill as possible."

"Oh," I meekly responded. I was convinced!

"And bring a large plastic bag!"

"Okay..."

I was in the field at precisely 5:01! But—I was NOT prepared for the scene that met me. The cow was definitely DEAD: blood was everywhere! The severed head and tail were lying discarded to one side of the cow. On the other side, the cow's skin was stretched out to dry. The bloody body was heaped in the middle, laying on a pile of dried leaves and grass. The meat department in Foodtown NEVER looked like this!

A man in a blood-stained shirt, wielding an equally bloody machete, approached me and gruffly demanded in Spanish, "*¿Cuántas libras? ¿Cuántas libras?*" How many pounds did I want? I was still stubbornly picturing my rump roast and steaks, and tried to direct him to the "appropriate" part of the cow. He just kept repeating, "*¿Cuántas libras? ¿Cuántas libras?*"

Getting nowhere, I finally blurted out, "*veinte*." Twenty pounds. He took his machete and hacked out, from who knows what part of the cow, twenty pounds of meat—and bone, and sinew, and what ever else was there! He took my plastic bag and dumped the twenty pounds of whatever into it and took my money. Blood was oozing from the bottom of the bag!

Where was the plastic-wrapped, hygienically-sealed, styrofoam-packaged beef of the U.S.? Where was the label that told me what part of meat I had bought? Where were my cooking instructions, and desired entree complements? Help! This was absolutely foul! I was quite certain that my bag didn't even remotely contain a T-bone or sirloin steak, or a rump roast. What did I do with this now? My impulse was to throw the whole mess away. But even in just a few weeks I had learned that food was a more precious commodity here than in the U.S. And besides, the thought of five more weeks of JUST beans sobered me quickly.

I took this "mess" home and put it in the sink. I began separating the good meat from the "whatever." This had been a wild cow. Its meat would be too tough for anything but ground beef. So I started grinding the meat... and grinding... and grinding... and grinding. The meat still felt warm to the touch, and bloody, and slimy. I lost my breakfast. I kept on grinding. I lost last night's supper, but I kept on grinding. By the time I was finished, yesterday's lunch and breakfast also left me in disgust!

That night I was determined we would have good, old, American-style cheese burgers for supper. I even managed to get two potatoes for the French fries. This would be a welcomed change from the usual beans and rice, and the boys came eagerly to supper. In spite of the day's ordeal, even *I* was looking forward to the meal.

We sat down, said the blessing, sank our teeth into this anticipated treat and chewed... and chewed... and chewed... and chewed! That meat was TOUGH! Tougher than shoe leather, tougher than reinforced steel. Ten minutes later we were still chewing! We hadn't even gotten the first bite down! It was so impossibly tough it would have been an excellent replacement for cement or steel. It could have even been used as an impenetrable material in atomic bomb shelters! But a hamburger, it was NOT!

In their prayers that night, in spite of all the strange, and confusing, and sometimes frightening experiences the boys were facing, I heard them thanking God for bringing us to Honduras. I was overwhelmed with their courage and trust in their Heavenly Father. I was struggling but they were flying with the wings of angels!

Our adjustment to third-world food supplies was not yet complete. Beans took the premier position in our diet, and the supply we bought in Tegucigalpa had quickly disappeared. So I took one of my plastic bags and went to the local *tienda* to buy ten more pounds of beans. They were fine at first. But after a few days some of the beans seemed to be moving. But it was probably my imagination. After a few more days, more beans appeared to be moving. No, they couldn't really be moving—could they? It only took another day for me to definitely know it was NOT my imagination. Those beans were having relay races inside the container, and pole jumps across the counter. When I boiled them, hundreds of black weevils floated to the surface!

I sorted through all the beans and threw out any that had "weevil holes" in them. Half my bean supply went in the trash. I was feeling a critical food shortage as it was. Within a week I had to buy more beans. And again, black weevils floated to the top when I boiled them. I tried skimming off the dead bugs as they floated in the boiling water. That worked for a time. But the weevil population kept increasing each day, and we had nothing else but those beans. It became impossible to sort bean from bug and so, on a memorable night, as the boys sat down to supper, Scott innocently asked, "Mommy, what are all the black things on the beans?"

I smiled sweetly at him, and brazenly lied:

"Pepper, dear."

> *Worship the Lord your God and his blessing will be on your food and water. I will take away sickness from among you.* Exodus 23:25

CHAPTER 18

Scorpions, Tarantulas, and Snakes—Oh My!

Ahuas was an intense culture shock! The bugs, the humidity, the heat, the flatness of the land, the Spanish language, the food, poverty, severe intestinal cramping and vomiting, and the time it took for mail to arrive—just to name a few things off the top of my head. The books that I needed for school hadn't arrived yet. But I was resolved that school would still begin the following Monday.

There would be eleven children in my little one-room schoolhouse. Isak, Ranée, and Klazien were my kindergartners. Janneke and Lucas were my first graders. Caleb and Erik were second graders, Kirstin, Corrie and my son, Chris were the fourth graders and Scott was the lone sixth grader. Ranée, Corrie and Caleb were the children of the MAF pilot. Kirstin, Eric and Isak were the children of the clinic administrator under the Moravian church. Janneke and Klazien were the children of a Dutch couple working with World Relief. Lucas was the son of a pastor with the Moravian church. He would be in my class only a short time. Janneke and Klazien spoke predominantly Dutch, and Lucas spoke the language of the natives, Miskito. It was an interesting mix.

The desks were hand made from rough lumber and were difficult to write on. The black board was wood, painted with a slate black finish. The whole appearance gave me the feeling that I had been jettisoned back 150 years to an earlier time.

School did begin that Monday, and praise the Lord, the books arrived just in time on an unexpected Sunday flight from Tegucigalpa.

Life fell into a comfortable routine. Teaching these children was a joy. They were all bright and eager students. Years of teaching multi-grade classrooms of special education children made it easy to teach five different grades of normal kids.

But there were a few additions to the classroom I never encountered before: scorpions, tarantulas, snakes, and bats!

Scorpions have a vicious sting. They loved to hide in dark, cool places such as inside desks, or in a child's knapsack, or behind the pencil sharpener. They could also be found in discarded shoes or in folded clothing. The children could never just reach into their desks to pull out a book. They first had to visually check the area, do the "scorpion shake," and then when nothing moved, reach in gingerly and pull out the desired book or pencil. Scott rode for two miles on his bike with a scorpion by his neck, hanging onto his knapsack. Once stung, you give scorpions ample maneuvering room.

Tarantulas also liked to visit our classroom. They were slow moving creatures, and except for their ugliness, didn't seem to pose much of a threat. One day little Ranée was coming to class, rather late, and by her demeanor, didn't really want to come that particular day. She had stopped on the dirt path leading to the school and wasn't going any further.

"Ranée," I called, "Hurry up. You are late for school. Come on!"

"I can't," she called back, and lisped, "There'th a taranthula on the path."

"Walk around it, Ranée. The field is plenty big enough for you to find a safe detour around him," I chided.

"I can't. There'th a taranthula on the path and I'm thcared," she piped back. She appeared as scared as apes are of bananas.

"Walk around it, Ranée!" I attempted to order.

She was bending over examining the big, black spider with absorbed interest. "No," she countered again. "I'm thcared."

"Ranée, do you want me to come out and kill him for you so you can come to school?" I coaxed.

"Yeth," she halfheartedly responded. She was not all that eager to come to school. "I'm thcared. There'th a taranthula on the path."

So I came out of the classroom with ten other children following enthusiastically behind. In my hand was my trusty tarantula killer: a hammer!

Ranée was still bending over the spider with rapt attention. The thing hadn't moved for the past ten minutes. Fear was absolutely nowhere to be seen on this child's face. But never the less, I responded as the "hero" adult on the spot. "Move back Ranée. I'm here to save you from the big, bad tarantula."

But she was now surrounded by ten other interested faces and wasn't about to lose her front row seat to what ever was going to happen to the bug. So I pulled back my hammer, and landed it squarely in the middle of the tarantula's back. Being a rather large bug, it squished quite nicely and its guts flew everywhere—but most of them found their way on to Ranée's knee.

In sheer revulsion, Ranée jumped back, hopping from one foot to the other trying to shake off the goo on her legs. "Oh groath!" she sputtered. "I've got taranthula gutth all over my kneeth! Oh groath! Oh groath! Oh groath! Now I can't come to thcool. I've got taranthula gutth all over my legth."

It was a lost cause. Even after washing her legs with water, she wasn't convinced that some eternal wrong hadn't been done to her. She wasn't sure if she could EVER return to school. But fifteen minutes later, when she found things kind of dull with everyone else back in school, she rejoined the class.

As I said before, tarantulas were more of a nuisance than a threat.

But snakes were a different matter. I was told that ALL snakes in La Mosquitia were poisonous. It was a point I didn't wish to argue with any one particular snake. During recess one day, the children were playing with discarded lumber and attempting to build yet another fort. Suddenly, to my horror, I saw a large viper coiled around one of the boards a child was about to pick up. "Drop it!" I screamed. "Get away from the wood, all of you! Right now!" Without question they all moved back. The snake sprang into the air, then slithered away into the deeper recesses of the pile. No one was hurt. I had the wood removed the very next day.

A month later we sat in church as a fer-de-lance (what the locals called a *barba amarilla,* "yellow beard") crawled about on the beams above the pastor's head.[1] He knew the snake was there but seemed to have little concern. He went on with his message from God's word and ignored the slithery visitor. I can tell you he had more faith in God's protection that day than I did. He might have been ignoring it but I was watching it enough for the both of us! For two hours I kept precise vigil on its whereabouts. I have to confess I can't remember a thing about the sermon. I did marvel at the Pastor's calm fortitude. When church was finally over and most of the people had left, me being one of the first, he climbed a ladder and captured the snake in a burlap bag and deposited it out in the marsh.

---

[1] See a photo of the church interior on page 124.

Only a few days later I noticed a brightly colored "worm" on the path. It was no more than seven or eight inches long and banded in orange, yellow, and black. I called to a Miskito man and pointed to the "pretty worm." He shook his head in terror and told me it was a coral snake!

And bats! The bats that did their nightly maneuvers in combat boots in my attic and walls didn't feel obliged to restrict their activity to just that side of the building. Periodically they would fly into the classroom in broad daylight—I'm sure just to scare the living daylights out of me. I have never been afraid of spiders and bugs and worms but bats will send me into a panic. It turned out a colony of hundreds of bats lived in the rafters of the little house and school! Nothing but bats would send me, a perfectly sane woman, screaming down the schoolhouse steps like a banshee, shouting, "*¡Murciélagos, murciélagos! ¡Ayúdame Joél! ¡Murciélagos!*" Bats! Bats! Save me, Joel! Joel was a handyman around the missionary compound who did various odd jobs. As far as I was concerned he was there solely to protect me from the bats. After my spectacular bat performance was repeated a half dozen times or so, it was decided to take off the siding on the house and EXTERMINATE the bats. As one man pried off the siding, two other men stood below with baseball bats and "batted the bats" as they flew into the daylight. Hundreds of bats flew out and surprisingly a few even got hit but most swarmed right into the classroom! Swirling about like a mini-tornado, they were everywhere. I felt them eying *me* as the prime source of their current inconvenience. Being the brave missionary soul that I was, I crouched quivering and shaking under my desk with a garbage can over my head!

The siding was replaced and made to fit more tightly, and for awhile there was peace in the heavens above. But I just KNEW the bats were still out there somewhere, waiting...

You of little faith, why are you so afraid?   Matthew 8:26

CHAPTER 19

Ribsy

I first noticed the dog—or rather its tail, sticking out of the garbage drum in back of our house. It was the scrawniest-looking tail, sticking straight up like an exclamation mark, and for quite a few days that's all I saw of the dog. It must have liked what it found in the garbage though, for it quickly decided to "adopt" our house as its territory. The scrawny tail was attached to the ugliest looking dog I had ever seen in my life. It was unbelievably skinny, almost starved. Every single rib was silhouetted along its side. Its stomach and backbone were so close together they appeared fused. The coat was an indistinguishable color, brindled with mud and soot, with fur that couldn't decide which direction to go. Its ears flopped down and gave the dog a pathetic, woe-begone look. The eyes were too far apart and too small for its face. In fact its whole head was too small for the elongated body. The elongated body was a mass of moving fleas and blood-swollen ticks. It bore absolutely no resemblance to the pampered creatures we call dogs in the United States. This was a third-world stray, accustomed to having sticks and stones thrown at it, and to surviving on what was left over after a half-starved human population had picked through the already-meager food available. I doubt if a kind word had ever been said to it in its entire life.

And so, because of my "elite" garbage—and whether I wanted it or not—the dog had parked itself outside my house as a permanent addition. It patiently waited for me to bring my daily offerings to the big oil drum. It never got in my way, and always waited for me to be quite a ways off before it would jump into the can to partake of its breakfast. The dog became a convenient garbage disposal and I started just throwing the leftover scraps on the ground for it, an arrangement it totally enjoyed as well. We called the dog "Ribs" for obvious reasons, which then became "Ribsy."[1]

An unspoken pact was formed in Ribsy's mind. I would provide

---

[1] Photos of Ribsy are on pages 118 and 119.

food and in return it became our "watch dog." Whenever the boys took off on their "expeditions" Ribsy was there, leading the way and sniffing the trail for danger. Wherever I walked, Ribsy was there chasing things I didn't even see away from my path. On school days Ribsy watched the school children playing in the yard. At night Ribsy guarded the steps of our house. Ribsy was a loyal sentinel, on duty twenty-four hours a day.

Ribsy, we soon discovered, was a girl—and pregnant! The belly that had been plastered to her backbone was now bulging and sagging with the weight of the pups growing inside her. She stopped her constant activity, and preferred to lie all day in the shade under the house. Her belly got unbelievably huge, and then, one day, she was gone.

The children looked all over Ahuas for her. They asked everyone if they had seen the dog. No one had. No trace of her could be found. She had gone someplace private, we guessed, to have her pups. And we would just have to wait for her to come back when she was ready.

Two weeks later Ribsy was ready. She presented herself in our yard just as suddenly as she had left, hungry and very much thinner. She danced around the children, then trotted off, only to look back and return. She kept repeating this maneuver over and over again. None of us were quick to catch on. But finally we did understand that she wanted us to follow her. A procession of nine children and one adult trailed her down the path as she barked and leaped excitedly. She led us along a dry twisty creek bed, through a field of prickly burrs, under half a dozen Miskito huts, down one windy, dusty rut and up another until she quite inexplicably stopped. It looked like she had led us on a wild goose chase. The area was completely deserted. We saw nothing and heard nothing. Ribsy lifted her head and sniffed the air, then sedately walked over to a discarded pile of wood and gently nuzzled something inside. The wood burst to life: puppies! Ten dark little squirming puppies, hidden in the crevices, wiggled and groped blindly for their mother and she now fully occupied herself with them. Proudly she nestled down and began to nurse them, making sure we were there to dutifully admire her offspring.

I *couldn't* leave the pups in the wood pile! Probably Ribsy had had dozens of litters of pups and cared for them in this same place quite efficiently. But my "refined" mind thought that this would just not do for these little things. Scott found a rickety cardboard box seemingly from thin air. Carefully we placed the wiggling little pups into the box and started our return procession: nine children, one adult, one box of squealing puppies and one Very Concerned mother dog who kept trying to jump into the box and check out her kids! We went back down the same rutted paths, crossed over streams, ducked under the huts, and found our procession growing and growing with each shack we passed: nine children, one American adult, ten squealing little pups, one Very Concerned mother dog and twenty laughing, *hysterical* Miskito men, women, and children. They were waving to still others to join them, gleefully pointing to the box, and me—and Ribsy, who was now dangling half in and half out of the box, her feet furiously treading thin air. By the time we reached the school yard gate, half of Ahuas was parading behind us, absolutely rolling in the grass with laughter. I didn't think the situation merited all *that* much attention! I tried to muster up some remaining dignity but it was pretty hard to do with the town's ugliest dog, back-paddling thin air, climbing over my head, trying desperately to get into the box and reach her squealing brood! I put the whole menagerie down in the shade of the schoolhouse. Ribsy was immediately in the box checking each and every one of her little ones from head to toe. When all were accounted for, and no serious injury discovered, she nestled down in the cramped quarters quite contentedly.

And so we now had Ribsy and her whole little doggy family living in the breezeway outside our door.

Ribsy's devotion to her family was phenomenal. She watched over them, guarded them, licked them, and let them nurse whenever they wanted. She would close her eyes in half slits and endured patiently their rough tugging and pulling and jostling for position as they nursed. One evening one of the puppies fell off the porch and landed in a heap. Ribsy stood over the puppy and howled. Her howl would have made windows shatter (if only there had been any window glass in Ahuas). She howled and howled and howled and did not let up until I came back from clear across the other side of Ahuas. When I came into the yard she ran up to meet me, took hold of my skirt and literally dragged me to her pup! She whined and whimpered and pranced, wanting me to "fix" her puppy. The little thing had broken a leg and was whimpering in pain. I nestled it in a towel and placed it back in her box. Ribsy was completely attentive to the poor thing all night.

The next day I took the puppy over to the clinic where a doctor benevolently volunteered to splint the leg for me. Ribsy followed all the way to the clinic door but stopped dead at the entrance. The doctor took the pup, placed it on a table and began probing gently the injured area. The pup, however, started an ear splitting racket, yelping and squealing and howling in pain as the doctor attempted to straighten the leg. Right in the middle of the racket, in the pristine operating room, Ribsy made her appearance! She had never entered a human's structure in her life but there she was, absolutely wired with concern and worry. She attempted to jump up onto the table to reach her pup, which started a whole panic with all the nurses in the room. Now added to the pups squeals were the nurses' shrieks and the attendants' frantic "shoo, shoo, shooing," all in an attempt to chase Ribsy out of the room. But no way was she going to leave without her child. I grabbed her around the neck and tried pulling her away only to have her break loose and set up a reverberating round of barks and howls of her own. The doctor had no other choice but to wrap up the pup's leg with the full assistance of Ribsy, who had now managed to scale the table and was meticulously checking out the doctor's every move! The nurses were still squealing and the attendants were still "shoo, shoo, shooing," but in spite of all the confusion somehow the thing was managed.

I carried the splinted and bandaged puppy out of the clinic with Ribsy close on my heels. She stuck to me like glue, jumping up every third step to inspect her child, all the way back to the house. When I placed the pup down, Ribsy, in utter relief, wrapped her body around the little thing, shielding her protectively, and ardently licking her. The puppy whimpered and sighed, then fell asleep in the shelter of its mother.

As the pups grew, they began to need something more substantial in their diet than just mother's milk. Ribsy had been taking care of litters of pups long before we came on the scene. She had the whole thing under control but I wasn't quite ready for her methods. She would devour any and all food she could find, then return to her pups and—vomit the whole mess up for them to enjoy! Yuck!

The puppies, however, thrived. They got to the stage where they could eat regular food and Ribsy, the ever devoted mother, scoured all of Ahuas for just the right morsels. One day I caught sight of her running across the field with a red plastic bowl clutched in her mouth. A heavy-set Miskito woman was running behind her and must have been shouting Miskito obscenities, but Ribs was way ahead of her and adroitly lost her. When I came up onto the breezeway I saw the red bowl in the middle of ten hungry pups—and in the red plastic bowl was about two pounds of chopped hamburger meat, worth an absolute fortune in local currency! The pups were thoroughly savoring this delicacy under the protective watch of their mother. I, however, was now harboring a *criminal!* Ribsy was a skillful and unrepentant thief!

The puppies grew and were old enough to manage on their own. Homes were quickly found for all of them except the little pup who had broken its leg. We kept it and named it Ginger.

Ribsy resumed her post as twenty-four–hour sentinel. She again was our shadow where ever we went. She watched over the boys as they played, and over me as I traipsed along the paths. She faithfully guarded our house each night. When we were away she would greet our return with a frenzied barrage of tail waggings and yips, and would make the most hideous looking "grin" to welcome us. The same devotion she gave to her little family of pups was now fully transferred to us. I found myself wondering how many times she had chased away some danger we weren't even aware of, or protected us from some harm that was avoided. I was a single woman with *my* little family alone in a foreign wilderness. I had no means to protect myself or knowledge of the dangers. Yet God had sent this dog, a very ugly dog, to watch over me. We think of guardian angels as glowing beings with long shining hair, translucent wings and a flawless countenance. Just maybe, though, guardian angels are the mundane, the ordinary, even the ugly—whose glow comes not from their outer appearance but from the qualities that God has given them of love and loyalty and devotion. They are there when we need them, ask nothing from us, and give to us all they have. Just maybe.

CHAPTER 20

The Eye of the Storm

For a solid week the rain pelted and pounded on the tin roof above us. The clatter was so loud I had to shout for my students to hear me. The wind banged on the jalousie windows and whistled through the cracks. A shallow lake of muddy swamp water surrounded the little schoolhouse and the wind pushed small rippling waves up against the bottom step of the school. It was hard to concentrate, hard to teach as the wind and rain assaulted us daily.

On Friday afternoon, as the children left school and sloshed home, I looked at the sky apprehensively. A supply flight to Brus Laguna was scheduled for the next day, and Diane and Barbara (along with their daughters) had invited us to ride along. Brus Laguna was a small village on the Caribbean Coast. It barely rated a dot on the map but I was excited about the prospect of our first trip outside Ahuas since we'd arrived. But if the rain kept up Tom wouldn't be able to fly the plane. Right now, the heavy clouds held a vise-like grip over Ahuas.

Saturday morning I awoke to the all too familiar rat-a-tat-tat of rain on the roof. The mosquito netting swirled like an eerie specter in the soggy gray light of dawn. Disappointment wrenched the pit of my stomach. Our suitcase was already packed and waiting by the door, but the flight didn't look promising. Clouds hung thickly on the horizon.

We waited and prayed for a clearing. At 10:30 the rain let up and the clouds broke. A single ray of sunshine poked through the mist. That was good enough! Tom gave the signal! We were off.

The Cessna followed the winding Patuca River north toward the coast. However, with each mile north, the wind grew stronger and the rain more forceful. The little plane danced about uncertainly in the relentless wind currents but precariously held its course. Ahead we saw the coast. It wasn't the usual serene blue vista: hundreds of white-capped crests bobbed and skated in the ocean below. Angry blue-gray waves smashed the beach. The palm trees shook like erratic pompoms. Tom was heading for the landing strip but it was no longer there! Brown swirling water engulfed the area.

He continued to descend. I didn't see any land, but he still continued downward. I braced for a crash as the wheels came in contact with the surface of the water. The Cessna touched down, swayed from side to side, sashayed, and hydroplaned recklessly across the deluged field. The plane careened towards palm trees and huts. The wind slapped the plane broadside and then—the wheels found ground beneath the water and held. We rolled to a stop with a fanning wake trailing behind us.

We hiked three miles to town, bringing the supplies the village needed, on roads that were flooded eight to ten inches deep. We smelled the town before we saw it. A stench of animal dung, stagnant mud, and human waste assailed us in the fading light. The closer we got to town, the stronger the reeking odor. The deluge of rain had caused the outhouses to overflow. The smell was almost unbearable.

On arriving we were met with an ominous warning: "There's a BIG hurricane in the Gulf and it's heading in this direction." Fear grabbed me with these words. I wanted to go back home but dusk was falling. MAF planes don't fly after dusk. We had no other choice but to find a place to stay and... and... and what?

We were led to a boarding house for high school students. Most of the students were home for the weekend so the building was empty. It was a rough, unpainted, wood structure with large windows but no screens, and ten or more beds against the wall that were just boards on four posts with sheets thrown over the hard wood. There were no mattresses, no pillows, and no electricity—just darkness and the penetratingly foul order of raw sewage. The wind was howling outside and the stench was everywhere. I stood in the middle of the room, staring about, trying to adjust my American expectation of comfort into this spartan Honduran surrounding. Scott and Chris had claimed beds in another room and seemed unfazed by this new adventure.

My dismal thoughts were interrupted by a small woman. Surprisingly, word had reached the town ahead of our arrival that *americanos* were coming. In spite of the storm, a supper had been cooked fit for dignitaries, in true Honduran style, and this woman had come to announce supper was ready.

Beans, rice, and rolls were placed before us on a long table. But the foul smell from the outhouses had caused my stomach to churn and wrench. Scott and Chris were looking equally green about the gills. The woman profusely expressed her pleasure in having the honor of *americanos* eating at her table. Meat was not a normal part of the

Honduran diet. It was reserved for special occasions. The hostess explained that, on such short notice, she had difficulty finding meat to honor our visit, but she HAD MANAGED, she confirmed proudly! She then produced, with a flourish, a plate of GREEN meat and generously placed large portions on our plates. It smelled the same as the stagnant water outside. My stomach was reeling, the stench outside was suffocating, and now in front of me was this green meat! The hostess was avidly waiting for me to "dig right in" and enjoy every succulent mouthful. I looked about the table. The local children were eying our large portions with envy.

"You have prepared a wonderful meal," I said to the woman, smiling. "What is this delicious meat?" I was afraid of her answer, well aware that I was expected to eat the entire portion on my plate.

"Turtle," she answered back, beaming. "Boiled turtle. Do you want more?"

"No, this is more than enough," I replied truthfully. "Thank you so much."

I looked at Scott and Chris who had simultaneously heard the identity of the "mysterious green meat" on their plate and were now pleading *desperately* with their eyes for an escape! I looked at the Miskito girls, again, who were still eying our portions enviously.

"Oh," I said with forced concern. "You have so little and we have so much. Let us share this delicious meat with you," I said with faked generosity. I piled my portion as well as Scott's and Chris's on one plate and passed it around to the ten girls. They attacked the meat greedily as it passed them. By the time it got back to us there was very little meat left, to our genuine relief. This we divided and attempted to eat, mostly by hiding it among the rice and beans. Any other day I might have been up to the culinary challenge. But the storm, the mud, the ooze, and the stench combined forces to undermine any rash experimentation.

We returned to the boarding house and prepared for sleep. Scott and Chris had been staunch troopers the whole day. We prayed together in the candle-lit room. I did not know where the hurricane was or where it was heading or how much worse it was going to get. I felt nauseous from the odor. And fear from the uncertainty was trying to fight for control. I was faced, again, with the unknown, and only God could I call to for protection. "God, protect us from this storm. Watch over us. Watch over this little village and the people that live here. You have always been our refuge. Be that for us now. Amen"

The boys fell quickly asleep. But I laid awake, feeling every rough groove and splinter on the entire length of the bed. I had intended to use the blankets as padding over the boards. But the chill air made them necessary for warmth. My bones rebelled against the hard surface and I ached everywhere. All night long I listened to the wind storm through the small village and the rain beat in torrents. The palm branches rattled and rustled as in a childish tantrum. I could hear objects being blown about and crash against each other. The building swayed and groaned. As fear tried to surface, I sang a hymn softly to myself, a hymn I had learned only a year before.

> *Anywhere with Jesus I can safely go.*
> *Anywhere He leads me in this world below.*
> *Anywhere without Him dearest joys would fade.*
> *Anywhere with Jesus I am not afraid...*

" 'I am not afraid....' Lord, help me to not be afraid. Help me to trust you, please," I prayed. I looked over at Scott and Chris. They continued to sleep peacefully. The tempest raged but they slept in the eye of the storm.

Sunday morning arrived, still shrouded in rain. Although I did not believe it possible, the stench from the sewage and stagnant mud was even stronger. But the wind had let up a bit.

We had breakfast an hour later: beans, rice, boiled bananas, and eggs.

Church began at somewhere around nine. When enough people piled into the small Moravian church, the pastor began to pray. He praised God for protection from the storm. He thanked God for His blessings and provisions. The congregation joined him enthusiastically, praising God together, in sincere gratitude. A shaft of sunlight broke through the clouds as he prayed, and beamed down on the bowed heads of these humble saints. The storm was over.

The people joyously sang in vibrant voices. The pastor preached. The people sang. Someone else preached. Someone else sang. Words spontaneously were shared from the Bible. The language alternated between Spanish and Miskito in rapid succession. I did not understand vast portions of what was being said but my heart responded in shared love and joy for Our Lord and Savior that transcended all language barriers. More singing, more praising, more preaching, more singing—until the final benediction was given and church was over. It was after one o'clock in the afternoon but no one was in a hurry to leave.

The sun was vibrantly shining. Tom would be able to fly the Cessna. We packed our things and prepared to walk the three miles back to the landing field but somehow a "taxi" had been procured, an old relic of a car. We piled in and bounced, jostled, and groaned all the way to the airstrip. The little plane's engine whirred to life. We could go home now—*after* the danger had passed, *after* the storm had raged, but also *after* we had witnessed God's protection.

Anywhere with Jesus I can safely go...

Would I ever really believe those words and *trust* first, rather than quake in fear first?

Anywhere He leads me in this world below...

Scott and Chris scrambled into the plane and fastened their seat belts. I climbed in after them. The plane ascended into the air, above the mud covered earth below.

Anywhere, anywhere, fear I will not know
Anywhere with Jesus I can safely go.

Lord, let that be my prayer and my praise. The eye of the storm is always in the palm of God's Hand.

You will not fear the terror of night,
nor the arrow that flies by day...
If you make the Most High your dwelling—
even the LORD, *who is my refuge—*
then no harm will befall you,
no disaster will come near your tent.
For he will command his angels concerning you
to guard you in all your ways.   Psalm 91:5,9–11

105

CHAPTER 21

The Ninevites

The little one-room school was in full swing. My kindergartners were learning their ABC's. My first graders were learning to read. My second graders were learning addition and subtraction *with* regrouping. My fourth graders were learning the finer points of reading comprehension and writing skills. My sixth grader had already finished the assigned sixth grade curriculum and was in the process of teaching himself algebra. We had published a school newspaper and put on a Christmas play. All this while the rain had beaten down incessantly upon the tin roof and bugs swarmed with every wind current that entered the classroom. The dry season was now beginning.

Schoolwork was the easy part of life in Ahuas. Doing homework by candlelight at first was a novel experience, then it became routine. The candle provided its own bug control as the flying insects were drawn to the flame then hissed away into an ignited oblivion.

Social relations were more of a challenge. Even the most "saintly" of missionary kids can act just like ornery, ordinary kids at times. When we arrived in the village the children there had already made firm bonds of friendships. Kirstin and Corrie, both almost the same age, were inseparable. Caleb and Erik, also about the same age, were a unified team. Isak and Ranée, the same age but different sexes, still seemed to be a fearsome twosome. Scott and Chris did not neatly fit into the social order.

Scott, however, absorbed himself with books and with his battery-powered computer. He never seemed at a loss in finding something with which to occupy himself. If he didn't fit in to some social structure, no big deal.

Chris was far more social and was resolved to fit in somewhere. He was the same age as Corrie and Kirstin but in fourth grade there is an unspoken understanding: *girls have cooties and boys are disgusting!* Caleb and Erik were two years younger but at least they were boys. So Chris directed a concerted effort to be their friends. Unfortunately the number "three" was working against him. Whenever he was with

JUST Caleb or with JUST Erik all was quite fine. But when Erik and Caleb AND Chris were together disharmony reigned. Usually the problem seemed to originate with Erik. He was fiercely jealous of his friendship with Caleb. Caleb was far more easy-going and congenial, even with Chris. This did not sit well with Erik. Added to this, Erik did not hold religious ideals very high. Talk of being "born-again" was not a concept his family embraced and being "saved" was foreign. Therefore, doing things a certain way to "please Jesus" went nowhere.

Frequently Chris would come storming into the house with his feelings hurt, angry with EVERYTHING. I would patiently remind him that he had a responsibility to return kindness for meanness. But my message was having a hard time getting through.

On one particular day Chris, having been excluded from Caleb and Erik's "club," was playing with little Isak. They had discovered a kind of village dump where there were all kinds of "treasures." Old chairs, tables, boxes, mattresses, and discarded wood. So with the help of a lot of imagination they were building a super-duper, colossal fort. All morning Chris and Isak had been working on their creation.

"Help me bring this wood over, Isak," Chris instructed.

"This is going to be a really neat fort, huh, Chris?" Isak bubbled.

"Yeah, and we can put furniture in it and maybe sleep out here," Chris continued.

"I might get scared."

"Don't worry, Isak. I'll protect you," Chris volunteered bravely.

"This is going to be the best fort in all of Ahuas, huh, Chris?"

"Yup, and when it's finished we can hide in it and no one will see us. It will be our secret. Come on, Isak, help me drag this mattress over to the fort. We can use it as the bed."

Lifting and lugging and building in the hot sun left both boys tired and thirsty. The fort was almost finished. In their eyes I'm sure it was the grandest fort in all the world.

"I'm thirsty, Chris," complained Isak. "Let's go to my house and get some juice."

"Okay. And we can bring back some more nails and a hammer to finish the roof," Chris added.

"And maybe my mom will let us bring back sandwiches so we can eat our lunch here. We could even eat it on the table in the fort!" Isak suggested enthusiastically.

So the two boys left their fort for awhile, full of plans and ideas of things still to do to make the fort even more fantastic.

Erik and Caleb had been spying on the two. They had watched as the fort had taken shape. Now it was left unprotected. Erik had a wonderful idea.

"Let's go and knock the fort down," Erik suggested.

"No, I don't want to," mildly protested Caleb.

"Come on, Caleb. I'm going to do it even if you don't help me. You're just chicken," taunted Erik.

"I am not!"

"You are too!"

"I am not!"

"Prove it then," challenged Erik.

Not to be left on a dare Caleb followed Erik, albeit halfheartedly, as Erik hit the fort with a vengeance. The walls were knocked down, the wood scattered about, and the carefully created "masterpiece" was quickly reduced to a ruined mass of splinters. As Erik was delivering his last mighty kick to a standing piece of wood, Chris returned. He had forgotten his thermos and had come back to get it.

Chris saw the two boys near the fort but did not fully understand what they were about.

"Hey!" shouted Chris. "Get away from our fort! Get away!"

Then his eyes took in the picture. There *was* no fort anymore, only splinters and rubble.

"What have you done?" he said as tears welled up in his eyes and the full comprehension of their action sunk in. "Why did you do it?" His words were choked in disbelief. "I didn't do anything to you! Why did you have to ruin it, Erik?" he sobbed.

Then anger took over. Chris charged Erik and Caleb in a rage. He caught them both briefly only to have them squirm out of his grasp and run away. "How could you do it?" he kept screaming as he chased the two boys through the underbrush of La Mosquitia. They were running for all they were worth, heading for Erik's house and safety, they hoped. Chris was close on their heels. But they manage to scramble up the steps just ahead of Chris and disappear behind the screen door.

Erik turned around and in a parting shot taunted, "You couldn't catch us. And your old fort was just a piece of junk!"

Erik's older sister, Kirstin, was standing on the porch as Chris yelled back to Erik, "You shouldn't have knocked down our fort! I'll get you back, you'll see!"

Then Chris ran home, tears streaming down his face. He barged through our screen door and fell on the sofa sobbing inconsolably.

"What's wrong, Chris?" I asked in alarm.

"I HATE him, Mommy! I hate both of them but especially Erik. I HATE him!

"There was no reason for him to do it other than just to be mean. It was just meanness, that's all it was! He was just being mean for no reason! I hate him!"

"What did he do, Chris? What happened?" I questioned.

Chris related the story as he cried and hiccuped, still bewildered why they had done such a mean thing. He mainly blamed Erik; Caleb had wrecked it a little but most of the damage had been done by Erik.

Just as he was reestablishing some control over the tears and hiccups, Kirstin stormed in through our door and glared at Chris. "You have no right to accuse my brother of knocking down your fort! He didn't do it! You shouldn't be chasing my little brother around! He didn't do anything and you better leave him alone!" With that she stormed back out and slammed the door in the process. A double whammy!

Chris fell back onto the sofa in a heap and started crying all over again. "I hate them, Mommy!" he wailed. "I hate all of them. I want to go home."

I kept my hand on Chris's shoulder as his sobs slowly subsided, stroking his head and silently praying for the words to comfort him.

"Honey, I know you feel real bad right now. It was a mean thing for Erik and Caleb to do. I don't know why they did it either. But I know that God's love has to be victorious over hate. Hate can't win, honey. As hard as it seems, you are going to have to forgive them. It's a very hard thing to do, Chris. But maybe, just maybe, God wants you to be the one to show Erik HIS love."

"I don't WANT to show Erik God's love! I don't care if he's ever saved!" sulked Chris.

"Chris, do you remember the story we were reading in class, yesterday, about Jonah and the whale?"

"Yes—why, Mommy?

"Because I think you're a lot like Jonah. God sent Jonah to save the Ninevites but Jonah felt about the Ninevites the same way you do about Erik. He hated them and wanted no part in bringing God's message of salvation to them. He ran the other way and what did God do then, Chris?"

"He sent the whale to swallow him and then dumped him on the beach near Ninevah," Chris mumbled.

"Yup, He knew Jonah hated the Ninevites but he still wanted him to tell them about salvation. I think that's what God wants you to do with Erik. Erik is your Ninevite, Chris." Chris was very pensive. His face and hair were damp with sweat. White tracks crisscrossed his face where the tears had made a path through the mud and dirt from the morning's endeavor.

"Hon, why don't you go and take a cool shower. It'll make you feel better," I soothed.

Chris disappeared into the little bathroom and soon water was splashing against the sides of the stall. I felt so bad for him. He had been trying so hard to make friends in Ahuas and just when it seemed he was making some headway something like this invariably happened. I had to admit I was feeling quite a bit annoyed by the whole situation as well. My very human, non-spiritual side was attempting to push to the forefront. I did not like the way Kirstin had presented herself a few moments earlier and was feeling a strong desire to give both those kids a piece of my—

My thoughts were interrupted as I caught the words Chris was saying in the shower. He was praying: straight-forward, honest and sincere. "I hate them Lord, but I want to do what YOU want me to do. I don't really know how. Will you show me God? Please show me. Show me how to forgive when I don't really want to. Show me how to love when I want to hate."

My little son was beseeching his Heavenly Father for help. Tears came cascading down my cheeks. For the first time my little one was asking God on his own for help.

An hour later there was a knock on our door. It was Caleb. He had come to ask Chris if he could borrow a book. He stood in the doorway, restless and ill at ease, visibly trying to tell Chris something but not sure how to begin. Chris quickly got the book Caleb wanted but before he gave it to him he addressed him in a voice filled with emotion.

"Caleb, I'm sorry. I'm sorry I was rough with you. Please forgive me."

"Chris, I'm sorry too." His words tumbled out. "I know you worked a long time on your fort. It was wrong of me to knock it down. I'm sorry, Chris. Really I am. I'll help you build it back up if you want to. Okay, Chris?" apologized Caleb.

"Yeah, great! It would be fun to build it back up. We have to let Isak help too, okay?"

"Sure," agreed Caleb.

Caleb returned home with the borrowed book and Chris's face was absolutely glowing. A bit later Chris saw Erik playing alone near the schoolhouse. He grabbed some toy cars and started down the steps. Erik started to bolt when he saw Chris coming but Chris called to him, "I'm not going to hurt you. I want to apologize for being rough with you earlier today. I'm sorry, okay?"

Erik was a bit taken aback and didn't know exactly how to respond. He was a little suspicious that this might be a sneak attack. But Chris's sincerity broke through his wariness.

"I'm sorry, Erik. Will you forgive me?" Chris persisted.

Erik fumbled for words. He was the one who had done something bad but Chris was apologizing. God's conviction fell on him, powered by prayer, I'm sure.

"I'm sorry too, Chris. I don't know why I knocked down your fort. It was a really neat fort."

"It's okay, Erik. You can help me make a new one, you and Caleb and me and Isak. It will even be better than the other one," urged Chris.

The two boys walked away arm-in-arm down the path. Chris had shown Erik undeserved forgiveness, God's kind of forgiveness. And God had helped him do it. Chris knew he couldn't do it alone so he asked God—and he found out God answers back. Praise God!

> *"Lord, how many times shall I forgive my brother when he sins against me? Up to seven times?"*
>
> *Jesus answered, "I tell you, not seven times, but seventy-seven times."*
> Matthew 18:21–22

Tegucigalpa, Honduras. Our arrival in the capital city for our initial stay at the home of Roy and Sue. Little did we know what was in store!

Ahuas, Honduras. An aerial view: The medical clinic is middle right; our house and school are in the left top corner, in front of the white house; and the runway starts at top middle, just above the two facing hangars.

Ahuas, Honduras. Moving in on our first day: Chris's face tells it all. This was our bedroom before the mosquito netting was up. The boys had the bunk on the left and my bed was on the right.

Ahuas, Honduras. Our home away from home: on the left was the school and the right side was our house.

Ahuas, Honduras. Our house/school is the red building in the middle. The director of the medical clinic lived in the white house in the foreground and an MAF pilot lived in the white house behind ours.

Ahuas, Honduras. The first time we saw Ribsy she was in the trash barrel behind our house enjoying our garbage. All we could see was her tail wagging from the top of the barrel.

Ahuas, Honduras. Ribsy after emerging from the barrel.

Tegucigalpa, Honduras. Scott standing in front of the MAF six-passenger Cessna.

Ahuas, Honduras. Tom's plane lifting off at the end of the MAF runway.

Ahuas, Honduras. A thatching party to make a roof for a church in a neighboring village. This was my attempt at tying the palm leaves together. The woman on the left was getting a real kick out of my efforts.

Ahuas, Honduras. Protestant Moravian missionaries were the first to evangelize the Miskito Indians; this was the Moravian Church in Ahuas.

Ahuas, Honduras. The church we attended and the beams in which the fer-de-lance snake crawled during the service.
(Story on page 93.)

Ahuas, Honduras. My two second graders doing reading lessons in the classroom. For one month I had a student teacher, who was just getting used to the Ahuas chiggers.

Ahuas, Honduras. Recess during the rainy season was held on the breezeway between the school and our house.

Ahuas, Honduras. Scott doing homework in our living room.

Ahuas, Honduras. United States Army helicopter landing in Ahuas during the Contra-Sandinista conflict. To the children it was a new toy.

Ahuas, Honduras. We went everywhere on foot or by bike. Chris was on his way to have dittos run off for the school.

CHAPTER 22
Jungle Camouflage

"Mommy, where are my camouflage shirt and pants?" pestered Chris.

"Hon, I think they're on the line drying. You wore them yesterday," I reminded him.

"Yes, but I need them again today!" he said emphatically.

"Chris, you can't wear them every single day! They have to be washed sometime," I informed him.

Just then Scott came into the house dressed in a damp camouflage T-shirt and long pants. "Scott, did you get them off the line? They aren't dry yet! You can't wear them wet," I said exasperatedly. Chris darted out the door and down the steps. "Chris!" I yelled after him. "You can't take them off the line either."

But both boys were gone in a flash disguised in wet military green. They joined Caleb and Eric, who were also similarly dressed. Together, they would disappear for hours, playing pretend war through the dry fields of Ahuas. Scott would make elaborate plans and strategies. Chris would build forts and barricades. Eric and Caleb would give the orders. They would hide and ambush, attack and run, and then fall down in the stubble laughing. Somehow this all could not be done unless they were suitably clothed in camouflage.

* * *

In March the weather was unbearably hot and dry. The only breeze that blew into the windows felt as if it came from a giant blasting furnace. The children lethargically entered the classroom, dawdling as they moved to their seats.

"Children, put your homework here on my desk. Clean off your area and hang your knapsacks on the back of your chairs. It's time to start the day," I instructed in my most official "teacher voice." Slowly my directives registered in their heads.

"Let's bow our heads and pray," I continued. "Dear Lord—"

I got no further. A loud buzzing sound zoomed over the school. All ten children had jumped out of their seats and were plastered to the windows, straining to see what was above them.

"It's a helicopter!" Caleb informed everyone excitedly. "A United States Army helicopter!"

"There are two of them, no three of them!" Eric corrected.

The helicopters had moved toward the landing field. One was about to touch down. Five little boys shot out of the door. Five little girls, ten paces behind, followed them. One rather sluggish teacher picked up the rear.

All three helicopters were on the ground as we neared the field. Twenty or thirty Miskitos joined us as the doors of the helicopters slid open. United States soldiers, dressed in olive green, jumped out. They were impressively armed, with military rifles and other battle paraphernalia.

"Wow!" Chris, Scott, Caleb and Eric exclaimed in unison.

One soldier stepped away from the group. He was clearly the one in charge. "Where is the hospital?" he asked the crowd. "Are there any Americans here?" He met with baffled looks as the majority did not understand a word he said.

"Can anyone tell me where the hospital is?" he repeated, to blank faces.

"The hospital is over in that direction," volunteered Barbara. "I'll take you there. My husband is the administrator of the clinic."

"How many other Americans are in this village?" he asked, relieved to find someone who spoke English.

"There are four families of American missionaries," Barbara informed him.

"How many adults, how many children?" He had a small notebook open now to record the answers.

"Seven adults, eight children and one baby," counted Barbara.

"How large is the hospital? How many beds? What kind of operating facilities? How are people transported in and out?" he read off from that same notebook.

"I'll take you there so you can see for yourself," Barb said calmly. "It's a small mission clinic built to serve the Indians of La Mosquitia."

Barbara, Diane and the sergeant disappeared through the crowd, which had grown to over one hundred people, all staring and pointing at the large military helicopters. Scott and Chris disappeared for a few minutes also, but returned quickly dressed from head to toe in their army camouflage clothes.

"Hi," said Chris to one of the men.

"Hi," he responded back. "You speak English?"

"We're from New Jersey," Chris said.

"I'm from Connecticut. What are you doing here?"

"My mom's a missionary. She's with MAF," Chris replied.

"What's MAF stand for?" the soldier inquired.

"Mission Aviation Fellowship."

"Your mom flies?" he said in astonishment.

"No, she's a teacher," Chris explained. "My dad flies though. He has an Piper Cherokee and he let me fly it once," Chris added, trying to impress the soldier.

"Is he a missionary too?" he asked.

"No, he lives in Alabama. My mom and dad are divorced," Chris said matter-of-factly.

"So are mine," said the soldier, who wasn't much past nineteen. "Stinks, doesn't it?"

"Sometimes, but sometimes it's okay," Chris said philosophically.

"Want to see the helicopter?" the man invited.

"Sure!" responded Chris. "Can my brother come too?" he said as he pointed to Scott a few feet away. "Scott, come here quick!"

"Okay. Come on, both of you. Let me show you this bird. It's quite a 'copter!" the soldier boasted.

To the envy of everyone in the crowd, Scott and Chris were ushered onto the large helicopter. The soldier showed them the control seat, the gadgets for finding direction, and those for steering. Scott was fascinated.[1]

"This helicopter is used mainly for transporting troops," the soldier explained. "I wish I could take you boys up for a ride, but I would get in big trouble if I did. You understand."

"Sure, that's okay. Why are you here?" questioned Chris.

"We're not supposed to say. Sarge says we're here looking for a place for R and R," he replied.

"R and R? What's that?" Chris asked.

"Rest and Relaxation," the soldier laughed.

"Here in Ahuas? You have to be kidding!" I interrupted, overhearing the soldier's response. "This would be the last place to look for that! We have a dirt volleyball court and a game every afternoon. But that's it. Look for yourself. You'd hardly call this a resort town!" I

---

[1] Photo on page 128.

said as I stretched my arm toward the flat, arid landscape dotted with thatched Indian huts.

"Volleyball?! That's good enough for me," piped the man. "Hey guys, you want to play some volleyball?" he called to the other soldiers standing around him.

With unanimous consent they moved to the volleyball court and within minutes an energetic game began, in spite of the one hundred degree heat. For the better part of the morning they took turns playing and resting, playing and resting.

Diane and Barbara returned with the sergeant. He joined in the game for a while until the heat got too intense. Then the men were ordered back to the helicopters. Off they whirled into the air.

"What was that all about?" I asked Diane.

"Beats me. The sergeant was extremely interested in the clinic. He asked all kinds of questions about how we would treat wounded and if we would treat *all* wounded," Diane replied.

"Why wouldn't we?" I asked.

"Well, some mission hospitals that treated national people or Contras have been attacked and burned down by guerrillas. If you treat one side, you make the other side angry. And if you treat the other side, this side gets angry. The Nicaraguan refugees have some pretty horrible stories to tell. Have you ever talked to Miss Mettie?" asked Diane.

"Yes," I replied, thinking back to Miss Mettie's account of how the Sandinistas had brutally murdered her husband, a Moravian Pastor, and their young son in front of her. She had barely escaped. The Sandinistas did not like the Miskito Indians, who were predominantly Protestant in a Catholic country. They were viewed as pro-Contra and thus persecuted by internal forces. Many of the Indians had fled over the border to Honduras for safety, Miss Mettie being one of them. There were stories of whole villages being executed by the Sandinistas. Miss Mettie had cornered me one afternoon a few months ago and urgently beseeched me to "talk to President Reagan!" as if I knew him personally. "Tell him," she begged, "that if the United States doesn't protect us, no one else will. Tell him!" she implored.

I thought of these conversations as I acknowledged what Diane was saying.

The next afternoon, and for quite a few afternoons after that, the helicopters returned. Scott and Chris, again dressed in camouflage, ran to greet the soldiers. The sergeant headed for the clinic and the men spontaneously joined the volleyball game that was already in progress.

"Hi again," said the same man Chris and Scott had talked to earlier. "My name is Bob. What's yours?"

"My name is Chris."

"I'm Scott."

"Hi, Chris and Scott. It sure is hot here. How do you stand it?" the soldier asked as he ran his hand across his forehead. Sweat was pouring down the sides of his face.

"It doesn't bother us. You get used to it," Scott said.

"What about these blasted gnats? They bite like fire!" he exclaimed.

"The chiggers? They itch like crazy in the beginning. My legs were a mess when we first got here but now they don't bother me anymore. Mom makes us put on this thick, oily, skin cream. It smells funny," Chris replied.

"Here, this is what the army gives us. See if it works any better," Bob said as he gave Chris a small green bottle of bug repellent.

"Why are you guys here? Where are you staying?" Scott asked.

"We're in the U.S. reserves on a readiness drill," he replied back. "Sarge says we'll be here one month. Boy, I sure can't wait for this month to be over! We're staying in a village, north of here, called Puerto Lempira, or something like that. It's a hole in the wall if I ever saw one! It's close to the Nicaraguan border." Bob explained.

"If you think that's a hole in the wall, why did you come here to Ahuas? This town is even smaller," Scott questioned.

"Because of you guys," the soldier quipped back.

"Us?" Chris countered.

"Yeah, in case we have to evacuate you," he threw out nonchalantly.

"Evacuate us! Why?" both boys asked incredulously.

"Oops, I've probably said too much. Forget I said that. Here, here's another bottle of that bug stuff. You can keep it too." Bob got up suddenly and joined his buddies in volleyball in spite of the heat he was complaining about.

I walked over to where Scott and Chris were sitting on the prickly grass. "Hi, boys," I greeted.

They eagerly showed me the treasure Bob had given them—nongirly bug stuff in an army green bottle!—and told me what he had said about evacuation. "What did he mean, Mom?" Chris asked with concern.

I wasn't sure. It gave their visits a more ominous tone. We did not know what was happening in the world around us. There was no TV or phone to keep us informed. No newspaper reached this far into the jungle. What was going on outside this little village? Why were the U.S. Army Reserves making such frequent visits to this isolated outpost two hundred and fifty miles from nowhere?

Diane and Barb sat down beside me. "Some Nicaraguan refugees have just arrived," Barb informed me. "They told Miss Mettie that the Sandinistas have crossed the Coco River and are attacking villages in Honduras. One village was trying to escape down the Coco River when the Sandinistas opened fire and killed all of them."

"Where?" I asked in horror.

"About forty miles from here," Barbara replied. "I was speaking to Hal this morning, on the ham radio. He says the U.S. has sent three thousand two hundred combat soldiers to Honduras. The news says the Sandinistas have 'invaded' Honduras," she continued.

"Invaded?!" we all repeated in shock.

"That's why the reserves are here and what the soldier meant when he told Chris and Scott we might be evacuated," I quickly figured out.

"A soldier said that to you?" Diane asked.

"He said it to the boys. He told them they were here checking out the village in case 'we needed to be evacuated.'"

But as we looked at the soldiers in front of us jumping and smacking the ball back and forth, they did not look like they were on a life-and-death rescue mission.

"Why is the sergeant so interested in the clinic?" I asked Barb, who had been giving the him daily tours of the grounds.

"For wounded," she responded. "I think he is referring to Army wounded. We are the only hospital for one hundred miles around and he is concerned about available medical facilities. He feels our clinic is too small and 'primitive.'"

The sergeant approached the volleyball court escorted by the clinic administrator and one of the doctors. The men immediately stopped playing and assembled themselves in rank. They were ordered back to the helicopters and within minutes the giant birds whirred off.

The helicopters didn't return after that. Over the ham radio we learned the 82nd Airborne Division had parachuted into Palmerola

Airbase in the center of Honduras. Hundreds of paratroopers dotted the sky as the news media avidly recorded the event. Why the planes didn't use the perfectly good runways to land their troops confused me. And Palmerola was two hundred miles away from where the Sandinistas were crossing the border. What good could they do fighting a border invasion from the middle of the country? But in the U.S., headlines appeared in the papers announcing "CONTRA COUNTDOWN," "SANDINISTAN INVASION," "REAGAN'S SHOW OF FORCE IN CENTRAL AMERICA," and "THE MARXIST CONSPIRACY."

Nicaraguan refugees, who had been slowly trickling back home, were once again pouring across the river. New arrivals appeared with stories to share with any who would listen.

In a few weeks the excitement died down. By the end of the month the troops left Puerto Lempira and returned to the United States. Ahuas was as before—except for the additional bottles of bug repellent my boys now had.

The threat of the Contra-Sandinista conflict that had frightened me in the months of preparation before we came to Honduras had actually occurred. There was fighting and war. But it did not come near us. The words God showed me in Isaiah, one anguished night last year, came back to me.

> *Tyranny will be far from you; you will have nothing to fear. Terror will be far removed; it will not come near you.... No weapon forged against you will prevail, and you will refute every tongue that accuses you. This is the heritage of the servants of the* LORD. Isaiah 54:14,17

I had been paralyzed by fear that night and God had reassured me with His words, "You have nothing to fear." He was now reminding me of those words and showing me He had been faithful to his promise. We were safe in the palm of God's divine care. How close we came to any real harm I will never know. Villages close by had been attacked. But God showed me to look with eyes of trust and know there was more than just U.S. soldiers protecting us in the jungle.

> *The angel of the* LORD *encamps around those who fear him and he delivers them.* Psalm 34:7

CHAPTER 23

Fire!

Half the year Ahuas was a swampy marsh. Constant rains nourished the lush vegetation and fostered the unrelenting swarms of bugs. The humidity was oppressive. The other half of the year it was a dry, brown wasteland, with cracked sod and brittle stubs of grass, a veritable tinderbox, fueled by a constant hot wind.

For weeks in April, distant fires had blazed across the parched land. Some days the burning brush sent smoke into our area so thick we could not see ten feet ahead of us. The days were engulfed in a perpetual dusk. Our eyes burned and watered. It was hard to breathe. I felt like I was standing in the middle of a roaring campfire with nowhere to escape. On Saturday the fire was half a mile away from our village. A fire ditch had been dug around our compound to keep it at bay.

We left for church early Sunday morning. Three hours later Diane and I and our children returned. To our horror we found the fire had vaulted the firebreak and was only twenty-five feet from the Moravian home. It was closing in on mine quickly. No one else had returned from church yet. The wall of fire stretched a quarter of a mile around us. There was no fire alarm to sound or fire engines with massive hoses to call. There weren't even hoses of any type around. Armed only with wet towels and rugs we started beating back the fire. But the wind was so pervasive that each area we snuffed out quickly bellowed back to life. Each of us, two women and five children, beat and hit the fire. Tears and soot mixed on my cheeks. Scott and Chris, their blackening faces set in a determined grimace, continued to pound the fire. The chicken house exploded into a furnace of flames. Sparks flew and ignited new areas of dried grass. The wind now turned and began to blow the inferno straight towards my little house. The butane tank for the stove was only ten feet from the front of the flames. Any moment a massive fire ball could mushroom. Our two homes teetered on the brink of destruction.

I ran into the house and retrieved our passports and wallet. There was no time to get anything else. "Oh God, please help. I can't do it. There are only five of us and the fire is so much stronger than we are. God, please help!" I frantically pleaded. I went back to the yard dragging additional wet rugs and towels and hopelessly continued to swat the malicious orange serpent. Suddenly I turned around to see an unbroken line, fifty strong, of Miskito women and children armed with pine branches joining us. As they moved in unison they rhythmically beat the burning brush. The fire cowered under their demanding assault. Inch by inch, foot by foot, we battled the front back together for two hours until the flame had been beaten into submission. My body ached, my hands blistered, my eyes burned, and my face was black, but the fire was no longer a threat.

"Thank you Lord! Thank you, Lord!" I repeated over and over. I hugged the women who had helped and they laughed at my sable face. The fire was bigger than we were but God had sent help. It was bent on destruction but God had intervened. The vast charred landscape, curling whiffs of smoke, and acrid smell testified to its power but God is still stronger.

We collapsed in exhaustion on the steps of the little house, now encircled by a smoking ring. "God you have been there for me always. Truly you have placed a hedge of protection around me. Thank you, Lord. Thank you."

An hour later, however, the wind drove the fire towards the village from another direction. The house immediately in its path was the pastor's home. He was away and only his wife with their infant son was there. She was in the yard alone trying to fight the blaze with a pine branch. Scott, Diane, and I armed ourselves again with the wet rugs and towels and joined her. The grass was taller around her home and the flames more intense. A few minutes later we were joined by twenty other people but the fire was too hot and moving too fast to control. Scott furiously beat the fire. A reed exploded with burning sap and burnt his left palm. The fire around his legs blistered his feet and ankles. And still the fire progressed. One of the men hooked up an old tractor and drove into the flames. Back and forth he plowed into the heat, turning under the blazing grass. Back and forth he dug. Flames danced around the tractor and spurted high into the sky. As they licked the gas tanks on its sides, it looked like even the tractor was destined to be claimed by the fire. At times the man was lost from sight behind the flaring wall. And then the flames began to sputter. The inferno retreated. The soil smothered the advancing red tongues.

Night fell and the sky all around Ahuas glowed in an orange shimmer. The flames encircled the village for forty miles or more. But the village was an isolated island in a sea of black charred earth. Not one home was lost. Not one thatched hut had been touched. The flames still raged across the dry land but the wind was blowing away from Ahuas. The whole village joined together to thank God for His protection. How awesome God felt.

We were stripped of all the powerful man-made devices to battle nature. We had no means to equal the relentless power of the fire. Only God could we call to help. And He did. His power stood in sharp contrast to our weakness. There were no trappings of "civilization" to dilute the view of His awesome might. We toiled but we did not toil alone. He was beside us always.

Scott's hand and legs healed, with a tiny scar to remind him of God's providence in our time of need. With the first rain of the season the black earth sprouted into green. Flowers appeared. The rebirth of God's love resonated in the carpet of His creation.

> *How many are your works, O* LORD*!*
> *In wisdom you made them all;*
> *the earth is full of your creatures...*
> *When you send your Spirit,*
> *they are created,*
> *and you renew the face of the earth.*   Psalm 104:24,30

CHAPTER 24

God's Course: Trust 101

As I swung in the rope hammock, one afternoon, I thought of all that God had shown me. I had been in Ahuas ten months. I 'd left my job, my home, and my family to follow God's call. I was a missionary! A year ago I thought missionaries were people in books who stood right up at the front of the line as God's righteous. I was nowhere near the front of the line. I was hoping somebody would let me cut in on the end. A year ago I thought missionaries were flawless beings with barely-concealed halos. I was all too human with faults and fears and weaknesses. Missionaries were dedicated preachers who led whole villages to salvation. I was only a teacher who taught ten children about God's love—good, but hardly halo-worthy.

When I first arrived and surveyed the alien landscape, and pondered on my existence here, I boldly prayed to God, "Look, Lord, what I'm doing for you!" He quickly rallied back in my internal thoughts, "No, child. Look what I'm doing for you!" That was the truer summation.

Had I become any more righteous, any closer to perfection? No, I was still me. Still stumbling when I should have been trusting. Still hiding when I should have been boldly proclaiming. But God had become so much bigger!

I struggled with trust. Fear came so much easier. But God repeatedly held my hand and showed me His presence.

I feared the jungle but God showed me its beauty. I feared war, but God showed me peace. I feared fire, but God showed me protection. I feared the storm, but God placed me in its eye. I feared isolation, but in it I found His all encompassing Spirit. I feared living on so little money but God showed me his abundant riches. I had nothing and because of that I saw God provide everything!

Each month five hundred dollars of support came in faithfully, from people in my church and from other churches, from teachers I had worked with in public school, from strangers, and from friends and family. Five hundred dollars a month and never from the same people. I was unbelievably wealthy by Honduran standards! God provided.

I feared what my children were leaving behind. But in Ahuas I saw Tom hold my son's hand and teach him to play baseball. I saw Chris learn what a Godly man did—how he lived with his family and served His Lord. Chris watched as Tom played with his children and he joined happily as Tom embraced him in that circle.

"Tom is a good daddy, huh, Mommy?' he asked one night.

"Yes, Chris, he is," I confirmed, remembering his questions about daddies years before.

"I want to be a daddy just like him someday," he said with conviction. "I want to be a missionary and fly a plane, just like Tom."

"Chris, that would be great." I said as I hugged my little man in my arms.

I had feared that my sons would miss out on experiences only the United States could provide. Tom and his wife had reached out to our family and included us in each vacation excursion they took out of Ahuas. We saw the beautiful untouched beaches of the Caribbean, and the magnificent Mayan ruins in Copán. We shopped in La Ceiba, had Thanksgiving in the flower-filled Siguatepeque, visited San Pedro Sula, and swam at Tela. A world beyond our imagination opened up before us. Experiences! If I had ignored God's call how much my sons would have missed!

I feared sickness but after the third day in the village none of us were sick again, in spite of the strange places we visited, the amoeba infested water we drank, and unusual things we ate—bugs included.

Worship the Lord your God, and his blessing will be on your food and water. I will take away sickness from among you....
                                                                    Exodus 23:25

I feared a foreign culture, and God showed me my neighbor. Who had it been before? A couple in a house next door to mine? Or was it the woman in rags at my door now, asking for clothes for her son, or the father who needed medicine for his sick child? Or the little boy who needed pencils and a notebook so he could go to school? Or was it the woman whose husband had been killed by guerrillas and needed food? Or Nora, who did not have enough milk to feed her twins, and was forced to feed only one?

144

*When did we see you hungry and feed you, or thirsty and
give you something to drink? When did we see you a
stranger and invite you in, or needing clothes and clothe
you? When did we see you sick or in prison and go to visit
you?*
Matthew 25:37–39

I have seen you, Lord, in each of these situations and have learned
compassion.

*I tell you the truth, whatever you did for one of the least
of these brothers of mine, you did for me.*
Matthew 25:40

I feared for my sons' education. But God had, in advance, provided all the books and materials they would need. It took the boxes
five months to reach Ahuas but they arrived on precisely the first day
of school, by God's provision. Scott thrived with the freedom to move
at his own pace and was finished with the sixth grade curriculum by
Christmas. He proceeded to teach himself algebra and physics. Chris,
who had a mild form of dyslexia, had struggled with reading. But in
Ahuas, with no TV to watch, books became an important past time.
His reading soared.

I feared loneliness and God provided a friend. What would Ahuas
have been like without Diane? She had the gift of genuine hospitality
and all of Ahuas was accepted openly. Whatever the need, she would
reach out to help. Whoever came to her door she invited in. She loved
the Lord and strived to serve Him in all situations. My life was blessed
by her joy, her humor, her sensitivity, and her faith. I was glad to be
included as one of her friends.

Only the Honduran police caused her to stumble for a moment.
Their building—part army outpost, part police station—was located
next to her house and across from mine. The police were bullies and
menaced people with their authority. When they got drunk, which was
frequent, they would shoot off their guns in the air riotously while
yelling foul words in Spanish. The falling bullets would ricochet
around the compound and zing as they hit the tin roofs of our houses.
One whole night Scott, Chris, and I spent crouched under our beds as
the bullets whistled around us.

The radio was always an integral part of their celebrating. The
volume would be turned up full blast, and blare raucously way into the
early hours of the morning. Diane had stoically endured her neighbors

145

for months. But one night in May her patience snapped. The radio was booming. The men were hooting and yelling. A few gun shots had already been discharged, when Diane slammed out of her door, stomped across the yard, tramped up the stairs of the outpost, and marched right into the middle of their assemblage. She grabbed the radio from the man's hands and, with a mighty heave, smashed it to the ground five feet below. She never said a word but all drunken revelry stopped in amazement as they watched her small figure stomp back across the yard and into her house. Enough was enough!

Had I accomplished what God intended me to do? I taught ten children reading, writing, math, English, science, and social studies. But God taught me so much more! I learned right in the beginning that I was not here because I was so good or so righteous, or because I had reached any special plateau of sainthood. Far from it! I was here because this was where God could get my attention, away from the haze of American materialism and my stupid self-sufficiency. He wanted to show me He loved me. He wanted to show my boys that He was their Father. He wanted to reveal to us a God so much grander, so much larger, and so much closer than we could have imagined. And— he wanted to show me I didn't need to be afraid, that I could trust Him in all things. His love is eternal, His Presence ever abiding.

Three weeks later we climbed into the MAF Cessna to begin our trip back home. School was over and many of the families had already departed on summer furloughs. The plane slowly taxied down the dirt runway. Suddenly I wanted to stop the plane, to make it go back, to embrace what I had learned here one last time. I turned to look out the rear window as the plane accelerated, willing myself not to forget anything. Framed in the dust and swirling eddies I saw Diane and her children standing alone in the field, waving good-bye—and I cried. In profound gratitude to God, I wept.

> *Trust in the* LORD *with all your heart*
> *and lean not on your own understanding;*
> *in all your ways acknowledge him,*
> *and he will make your paths straight.* Proverbs 3:5–6

CHAPTER 25

The Celebrities in the Crowd

"Mom, do you think my friends will still remember me?" questioned Chris.

"Yes, I'm sure they will," I assured him.

"I'm afraid they might have made new friends, Mom, and not want me around anymore," he said worriedly.

"Chris, they might have made new friends but that doesn't mean they won't still like you," I said as I adjusted the light above him.

It was late at night. We were flying over the southern states, on our way home from Honduras. Scott and Chris sat on either side of me, darkly tanned from a year in the tropical sun. It seemed easier to reassure his fears and concerns than it was to appease my own. Would my job still be waiting for me? What condition would I find my house after being rented for a year? What money would I live on the two months before school started again? Would my car still work after being idle for a year?

But on the other hand, what would it be like to shop in a regular grocery store, drink water right out of the faucet, turn on electricity whenever I wanted, or call someone up on the telephone? Would I be startled the first time it rang?

Our plane was not due to land in Newark airport until almost midnight. The flight seemed long and somber. I was caught between the sadness of leaving friends behind and the anticipation of seeing friends ahead.

"Mom, how are we going to get home after we land?" asked Scott, interrupting my thoughts.

"I'm hoping Grandma and Aunt Dea have gotten my letter and will be there to meet us," I said.

"Will they have enough room for all our luggage?" Scott continued to inquire.

We were coming home with 15 suitcases and boxes. "If Grandma drives her motorhome to the airport, we'll have enough room," I concluded.

"Where will we sleep tonight?" piped in Chris, continuing to focus on his transition back home.

"We can't go home to our own house just yet, because the beds aren't ready and there's still a lot I have to do before we can move back in. We'll sleep at Grandmommy's tonight, okay?" I still was not sure if Grandmommy had gotten my letter in time. I would only know after we landed. I just hoped she'd be there!

"Okay. But I can't wait till we get back home, Mom. I want to see everybody," he bubbled, forgetting his previous concern.

The light came on announcing the final approach. Seats and trays were to be in their upright position. I leaned over Chris and looked out the window as the plane descended below the clouds. I was surprised by the flood of lights beneath us. For ten months we had lived in a world of candlelight and darkness. Even in the cities, electricity was not the norm. Only a faint flicker would light the darkened landscape. But below me now, *everything* was illuminated in a halogen orange glow. What a contrast between the two worlds! I continued to stare in amazement as our plane reached the runway. How wealthy the United States is in comparison to developing countries! It literally SHINES!

The plane rolled into the terminal. Sleepy passengers grabbed luggage and belongings as they embarked. In the late hour the airport was empty. The long corridor was dark and shadowy as we walked toward the waiting room. I was still uncertain who would be there waiting for us. I felt like a stranger, insignificant and alone, returning to my homeland. Scott and Chris lagged behind me, feeling the strangeness also.

As we approached the end of the hall, we noticed a flurry of activity ahead. Banners and streamers, balloons and noise makers engulfed an enthusiastic crowd in the waiting area. A rumor circulated through the passengers that there was a celebrity aboard! Who else would bring out such a large reception? I looked around quickly, trying to spot the "celebrity." I didn't want to miss anything important! I wasn't alone. Everyone was looking around for the "celebrity," too. Who could it be? We took a few more steps into the open room.

All pandemonium broke loose! "Welcome home, Cyndy!" the crowd shouted in unison. "Welcome home, Scott and Chris! Welcome home!" Whistles tooted, streamers rustled, and noise makers rattled. "Welcome home!" echoed the crowd again.

I was taken completely off-guard, surprised and flabbergasted, astonished and dumbfounded. It was midnight, on a Wednesday night, and sixty people from my small church had traveled in an old school bus just to be there and greet us as we came back home. They had planned our home-coming for weeks, with sign-up sheets and posters. Husbands and wives, parents with children, grandmothers, widows, and friends were there. I was so touched by their gesture, tears blurred my vision. I was speechless. Scott and Chris just stared in bewilderment. Only moments before we had felt alone and slightly abandoned. Now we were the "celebrities" in the middle of an embracing throng.

"Thank you for coming to meet us. Oh, thank you. It's so good to see all of you! It's fantastic! Thank you," I repeated through the tears in my eyes and the lump in my throat. "Thank you!" I wanted to hug everyone at once, however I was also embarrassed, unsure how to truly convey the joy and the gratitude I felt towards each person. "Thank you for coming. Thank you for caring." It sounded so inadequate.

The last ones to join the crowd were my mother and sister. Mom had gotten my letter but they had been waiting at the wrong gate for our arrival.

We were back home, among family and friends. We were back home but we had never really left the family of God. It just had grown bigger!

> *Enter his gates with thanksgiving*
> *and his courts with praise;*
> *give thanks to him and praise his name.*
> *For the* LORD *is good and his love endures forever;*
> *his faithfulness continues through all generations.*

> Psalm 100:4–5

CHAPTER 26

The Worry List

The first rays of morning were lighting the sky. Half-conscious, I reached out to push the mosquito netting aside, but my hand only grabbed air. I searched for the usual smell of mildew and sweat, but came back with soap and fabric softener. I listened for the roosters' early morning crowing and the plodding clop of the wild cows. But instead, the sound of cars driving past. A radio in the distance intruded disjointedly. I couldn't hear the gentle breathing of Scott and Chris beside me. Where was I? Nothing was familiar.

I looked about the room. A yellow chair was in the corner, a white dresser was next to me, and yes, there were the dolls still sitting on the bookcase above the desk. I opened my eyes, now fully awake. This was my childhood room, the room where I grew up. I was home in my mother's house. Scott and Chris were in a room of their own—my brother's old room—with clean sheets covering them, and a soft mattress underneath.

As I dressed, I marveled at the cleanliness of life in the United States. I turned on the bathroom faucet and stared at the stream of flowing water. I wouldn't have to boil it! I could drink it right from the tap and not worry about parasites. Both hot and cold water were there with a turn of a handle.

"Amazing," I thought. Then I laughed as I pictured myself being the only person, in all of New Jersey, up and this hour and standing, enthralled, in front of a spigot of clean, gushing water.

An hour later, we all sat down at the breakfast table. A flick of the switch and electricity was on. A toaster, rather than the oven, browned our bread. Boxes of American cereal, still crispy, lined the counter. Milk came out of a bottle and there were no ants in the sugar!

"Amazing." It was easy to offer a prayer of Thanksgiving to God.

There was much planned for today. For a year or more I had mentally carried around a "worry list." At the top of the column were four items: JOB, FINANCES, HOUSE, and CAR. Today I would discover the state of two of these, HOUSE and CAR. The "car" was at Dea's, and after reclaiming it we were going to head south for the "house."

Dea's van led the way on Route 80. Grandmommy, the boys, and I followed behind in Mom's bulky motorhome. For half and hour we cruised along without a problem. As we approached the city of Paterson, Dea's van inexplicably lost power. Cars whizzed by as she crept along at a blinding twenty miles an hour. Finally she limped to the shoulder of the road. The van shuddered, heaved, and a convulsed to a stop, unable to be coaxed even an inch further.

Between all five of us, the amount we knew about car mechanisms wouldn't fill a line of print. So we unanimously decided it would be best if Dea stayed with the van while Mom and I, and the boys, went in search of a gas station and mechanic.

Mom and I didn't have a clue as to exactly where we were going to find a mechanic so we chose the scientific method of "random search." The city streets of Paterson interwove together like a maze as we drove up one and down another. But we did eventually locate a station with a mechanic and a tow truck. However, the mechanic didn't speak English very well. I tried to explain to him our predicament and direct him to where Dea's van was parked. Still I wasn't sure he fully understood what I was saying. So, as his truck pulled out of the station, I jumped impulsively into the cab to better direct him to Dea's location. Mom followed in her motorhome.

Two blocks from the station the man turned and looked at me, moving his eyes from my face, down over my whole body. His look frightened me and made me regret my impulsive decision to get into his truck. He moved his eyes to the rear view mirror and looked at my mother's van following. A ugly grin turned at the corners of his mouth and his foot pressed heavier on the accelerator pedal. He made a sharp right, and then a quick left. He turned street after street in random succession. I knew we were *not* heading towards Route 80.

"Where are you going?" I asked. "Isn't Route 80 in the other direction? My sister is on Route 80." I said, hoping he just hadn't understood me initially.

He didn't respond but just kept driving chaotically through the city streets. A light turned red. He slowed but then continued through. "You aren't going in the right direction!" my voice trembled. "My sister is on Route 80! Please slow down!" my voice rising in pitch.

"You will lose my mother! She's following behind with my sons! Please slow down!" Fear gripped me as I begged.

I hardly hoped she was really still following behind. How could she have kept up? He turned another corner and darted down a side street. He looked again in the rear-view mirror and muttered something I didn't understand. I followed his gaze. There was my mother's motorhome, trailing his truck doggedly. She turned and swerved in sync with every turn and swerve of his. Every light he ran she followed in close pursuit. She was eighty years old and driving as if she were in the Indy 500! She sensed my fear, as only mothers can, and was positively resolved not to let his truck out of her sight. For half an hour his truck and her cumbersome motorhome weaved in and out of the streets of Paterson, in a macabre dance, stuck together as if conjoined. I hung onto the door, ready to jump the moment he slowed down. He looked again in his rear view mirror and muttered. He couldn't shake her.

His truck slowed down to the speed limit. He looked at me and said, as if nothing unusual had transpired in the last thirty minutes, "Your sister, she is on Route 80?"

"Yes," I said in a strained voice.

"We go to her now," he said flatly.

Five minutes later we pulled up behind my sister's van on the shoulder of the busy expressway. Mom stopped right behind him. I was out of his cab like blue lightning!

"What took you so long?" Dea called to us. "I was getting worried."

On the scale of worry, I don't think she came even close. I looked at Mom. Her face was ashen as she stood beside me, holding onto the side of the van.

The man casually strolled over to the van, adjusted a few wires, tapped on a the plugs, tightened something else, and the engine roared back to life. Dea paid him, oblivious to the events of the last half hour. His truck disappeared down the road.

The dreaded scenario that had terrified me never happened. I was standing safely between my mother and sister. My children were near by. The day was still bright and warm. Everything was so normal!

Did I just imagine his evil intent? Or was I spared, in God's grace, through a mother's persistent devotion that enabled her 80-year-old reflexes to drive at reckless speeds through narrow speeds, pursuing deviant tow trucks, because her daughter needed her? I put my arms around her and held her tightly, her small frame was still trembling. "Thank you, Mommy," I whispered, words that barely touched my gratitude. Her eyes looked back with a wisdom that understood far beyond the words.

All of us got back into Mom's motorhome. What a mess! The contents in her cupboards and drawers were strewn all over the floor. The interior looked as if a cyclone had whirled through, and couldn't find the exit.

"Mommy," Chris said as I sat down beside him. "That man drove like a lunatic!"

"Yes, he did, Chris," I confirmed. "But your Grandmommy drove like a Grand Prix Champion!"

A half hour later I found my own car snugly stored in Dea's garage. After the battery was reconnected, it started right up. "Worry item" number one could be checked off the list.

#1, CAR: survived and working fine!

The boxes and things in Dea's van were transferred to my car. Next destination: HOME!

An hour later Mom and I pulled off the Garden State Parkway, onto roads I couldn't believe I'd traveled on just a year ago. I was filled with reassurance as familiar sights and landmarks appeared, unchanged; constant, in spite of the changes our own lives had experienced.

For months my house had been a priority on my "worry list." I had dreams of coming back to it and finding it destroyed and in shambles, with windows broken and doors hanging by their hinges, swinging to and fro in the wind. The rugs would be ripped and stained, and the walls punctuated with gaping holes. I would always wake up from the dreams, begging God to watch over my house. But now I was about to meet prayer with reality. How was God as a landlord?

I pulled into the driveway of my small shore house. The tenants had only vacated the house a week earlier. From the outside it looked, amazingly, just as it did when we left. I unlocked the front door, braced for the onslaught of bats, rats, garbage, and the images of my night-mares to confront me. I stared—

The house was IMMACULATE! The carpet had been vacuumed, the walls scrubbed, the woodwork dusted and polished, and the kitchen positively *glistened!* I opened one of the cupboards. Each shelf was stocked with boxes and cans of food. The refrigerator was loaded with fresh milk, eggs, orange juice, produce, and meat. It was all absolutely beautiful!

There was a note on the kitchen table:

"WELCOME HOME!
FROM THE WOMEN OF THE CHURCH."

I looked around in astonishment. That feeling of tremendous gratitude swept over me again. Gratitude to the women in the church and especially gratitude to God. Yes, Lord, you are a very good landlord! Item #2 was now joyfully checked off the "worry list":

#2, HOUSE: survived and condition excellent!

Life quickly picked up the pace of normalcy and routine. I called the school district where I had previously been employed. "I'm back!" I informed them. "No, I wasn't eaten by a crocodile or attacked by a boa constrictor. Can I have my job back?" I barely managed to avoid pleading and begging.

"Yes," was the marvelous response. I was even given a choice of two positions: teacher of a special education class like the one I had before, or a new position as a second grade teacher. I had always wanted to teach second grade. Ecstatically I opted for the second grade position. Worry item #3 was checked off:

#3, JOB: better than before!

Only FINANCES was still on the list. I had two months to go before I would again be earning a salary. How would I pay the mortgage and handle the bills? If I had been paying attention I would have already crossed FINANCES off. But at times I am unbelievably slow at catching on. God was way ahead of me. The church had decided to continue my monthly support until September, even though I was off the mission field. Many of my other supporters and prayer partners also continued sending checks into September. Hesitantly, then with more conviction, I checked off the final item:

#4, FINANCES: God provided!

A few days later Chris's friends had a party to welcome him back home. He returned later that evening, smiling and bubbly from the festivities. He excitedly recounted all that occurred, the games they had played, the gifts they had given, and the things each one had shared with him. As he prattled on, a flash back entered my mind of his worried apprehension on the plane trip back home. He had been carrying the item FRIENDS on his "worry list."

"Chris, Honey. It looks like your friends didn't forget you after all. It seems like they still want you around for a bit longer," I laughed.

Chris hugged me, beaming from ear to ear, and an invisible check clicked.

FRIENDS: He watches over them, too!

Worries! Such a waste of time! I ought to tear up that "worry list" and toss it to the wind. Why do I always grab
>   the last jagged sliver
>   just before it vanishes
>   into God's eternal care?

Do not be anxious about anything but in everything, by prayer and petition, with thanksgiving, present your requests to God. And the peace of God, which transcends all understanding, will guard your hearts and your mind in Christ Jesus.   Philippians 4:6–7

CHAPTER 27

Grandmommy

On July fourth Grandmommy went into the hospital. She was having difficulty breathing. It probably was just a bad cold or her allergies acting up, she assured us. Mom was resilient. Nothing could get her down.

However, a few days later, with Dea and me beside her in the hospital room, the doctor sadly informed us that Mom's condition was quite serious. Her cancer had returned and both her lungs were severely affected.

"She had tests done—only three months ago," challenged my sister. "The results indicated she was cancer-free! How could her lungs be riddled with it so quickly?"

"The cancer has come back with a vengeance," he said gravely. "It is invasive and fast-moving." He proceeded to lay out the pros and cons of aggressive and of less-aggressive treatments. "Either way," he said dismally, "she has no more than three months to live." The prognosis was bleak.

It was Mom's decision to make. Did she want to go through chemotherapy and radiation treatment again? Did she want to attempt to beat the odds one more time? I wanted her to say, "Yes." I wanted her to fight back. Cancer had claimed Dad. I didn't want to see the same cruel victory drawn on my mother's frail form. I didn't want to lose her! "Please, Mommy," I whispered. "Fight back."

"No," she quietly said. "I'm eighty years old. I don't want to go through all that pain and sickness again. I miss your Dad. I miss him terribly, and I'm tired. I just want to go home. If I only have three months to live, I want to be in my own home—home where all my memories are, where each room is filled with forty-five years of love and happiness. I want to go home."

Dea and I vowed we would honor Mom's wish to keep her in her own home, even though we both had homes and families of our own to look after. Somehow, with God's help, we would do it. We set up hospice care, and made a schedule. I would stay with Mom from

Monday to Friday during July and August. Dea would stay with her on the weekends. When school began in September, we would switch. Mom, on her part, did not intend to slow down until she had to. With her portable oxygen tank, she went everywhere: to church, stores, and even the Jersey shore.

The summer was blistering hot. Mom had always hated air conditioning, but her breathing was labored in the high humidity. My church lent her a window unit which allowed us to keep one room comfortable for her. There she established her domain. Seated in a large over-stuffed chair by the front window, she was as regal as the Queen of England. Neatly arranged around her were her sewing supplies.

She was intent on finishing her contribution to the church's Christmas Crafts Bazaar. Twenty little mice people, dressed in fancy tuxedos, exquisite ball gowns, suspendered britches, and frilly summer frocks popped their little heads out from her sewing bag. Hand-quilted pillows were scattered on the floor.

Mom had always been extremely talented with a needle. Most of the dresses I wore growing up were hand-made, something I did not appreciate at the time. I remember complaining to her that I wanted clothes that had tags in them, like other kids did. So she stitched in a label with embroidered lettering: CUSTOM TAILORED WITH LOVE BY MOTHER.

Every Easter and Christmas I would get a new "fancy" dress. The whirring of her sewing machine could be heard through most nights, after everyone else had gone to bed, stopping only an hour before dawn. And surely, under the Christmas tree or near an Easter basket there would be a box with a brand new dress in it.

When I became old enough for formal proms, we'd look in all the most expensive stores until I found just the dress I wanted. She'd examine the garment meticulously, and go home to reproduce the gown flawlessly on her thirty-year-old Singer sewing machine.

My wedding dress was copied from a page in a bridal magazine. The only argument we had concerned the color. I wanted the gown in a soft ivory. She wanted it in PURE white, the PURE being more of a statement than a hue. But the gown (in pure white) was beautiful. The intricate lace appliques were sewn to the satin bodice with threads of genuine love.

She could do anything with her hands. Every piece of furniture in the house had been reupholstered at least four times. She furnished my brother and his new wife's first apartment with "finds" from road side trash that she redid in chartreuse and turquoise. It was a gift they were not quite sure how to accept!

There was nothing she could not sew. Curtains, drapes, slipcovers, costumes, doll clothes, and stuffed animals were all products of her artistic hands.

"Most things," Mom said, "are learned from necessity." That was certainly true of her cake-decorating skill. When Dea was married in 1958—also in a "mom-made" gown—all the important arrangements had been handled, from church reception to cake decorator. The only unforeseen complication was that the cake decorator was an alcoholic, who decided to go on a binge the day before the wedding. The cake was baked. The frosting prepared. However the decorator couldn't steady his hands enough to hold the frosting gun.

Mom, who had made ceramic roses, flowers, and figurines in her earlier days, took charge at a rather intense moment and decorated the five tiered cake masterfully, with pink roses, tapered green leaves, and delicate lilies of the valley. It was a work of art!

She was quite proud of her accomplishment and from that time on, at every special occasion, be it a birthday, Mother's Day, Father's Day, anniversary, or just company coming, we could depend on Mom to produce a five-tiered extravaganza of a cake, decorated with pink roses, tapered green leaves and delicate lilies of the valley. However, being a small family and not particularly fond of cake, there invariably would be scads of cake left over. Mom hated to waste anything, so the cake was stored in the back of the refrigerator, all two hundred pieces of it.

Months later, when the cake had achieved a decisively greenish cast and the texture could be a brick substitute, Mom would sweetly ask my unsuspecting friends if they would like a piece. Cake! A lure they seldom resisted but quickly regretted. I was convinced it was part of her secret campaign to keep me friendless through my teenage years!

So many things I took for granted: her talent, her devotion, and her love. She was always there. If I became scared or sick in the middle of the night, she'd be there. Even when I was fully-grown with a family of my own, she would get in her car, drive an hour to my house, and be there because I needed her, whether the time was two in the afternoon or two in the morning. Her strength and determination were indomitable, as was her love and devotion to her family.

Now she needed me and I would stay by her, whether it was two in the afternoon or two in the wee hours of the morning.

The cancer moved at an unmerciful rate. Mom, who had always been a petite woman and watched her weight, was at first delighted by the pounds that effortlessly evaporated away. But the weight continued to shed and food became an issue. Nothing appealed to her. She would only pick at her meals and dab at desserts.

School began in September. Dea and I switched schedules. During the week I taught second grade. The boys were now in seventh and fifth grades. On Friday afternoon, I would pick up the boys and drive to Mom's. Her needs were much greater now. Dea's nurses' training was a blessing. She cleaned and cared for Mom with professional skill. I came on Friday and sat by Mom's bed and talked. We talked of life, of love, of sorrows, of Dad, and of God.

"I wanted you to get married again," she told me. "I want you to know the same joy your father and I shared for fifty-two years."

"I know, Mom," I said. "It just didn't happen for me."

"I liked Cliff," she said reflectively. "Your face always beamed when he was around. I can still see the two of you, on the dining room floor, watching TV." She paused for a few moments, then continued, "I don't think I ever saw your Father so sad as he was in Texas when Cliff left."

"Mom, it was a pretty sad time, but it's over, and life goes on. It made me much stronger."

"Your Father was a good man. I miss him so much. I have been so lonely without him," she said as her eyes pooled with tears.

"I don't know if they make marriages, anymore, like you and Dad had. They exist only in dreams and wishes now," I reflected.

"You'll get married again—someday," she said as she drifted off to sleep.

As death came closer, her thoughts became clouded with uncertainty and fear. Death frightened her. Why didn't God heal her, she demanded. Why didn't we choose the aggressive cancer treatment for her? Why wasn't God listening to her prayers? She was angry and afraid. She had accepted the Lord as her Savior, but on her own terms, not His.

"Oh Lord," I prayed silently, "help my mother to accept you for who you are. Help her to trust you. Be there for her, Lord. Comfort her and let her feel your presence. Help me too, Lord. For I love my mom, and I don't want her to leave me. Oh, Lord, I will miss her terribly."

Mom weighed less than seventy pounds. I could carry her in my arms. Our roles had reversed. I was the mother and she was the child. I smoothed back her hair and kissed her gently on her forehead. "Mom, I love you." Tears fell from my eyes onto her pale, translucent face.

The leaves had changed color. Oranges, reds, golds, and yellows fanned across the front window as the wind scattered the wayward vestiges of fall. Mom slept most of the time now.

"When time stops I will no longer be here," she cryptically stated one day. She was intently watching the clock by her bed.

"Mom, I don't understand what you mean," I said, but she had fallen back to sleep.

She woke later, bewildered. "I'm still here," she said surprised. "I thought I wouldn't be." She slowly looked around the room. "I saw your Father," she continued. "He's waiting for me, and the clock had stopped moving." Slowly she turned her head towards the clock. "But I'm still here—and the clock is going again..." Her voice was tinged with disappointment. She was in no pain. Peace had replaced her anger and fear. She wasn't making deals with God, but trusting and resting in his gentle love. Her fear was gone because she knew when "time stopped" for her she would be with her Lord.

"Mommy, I love you," I said. But she, again, had drifted back to sleep.

Two days later, on October thirtieth, she passed away peacefully. Dad and Mom were back together. She didn't have to be lonely anymore. The Lord held them both in His eternal light.

Mommy, I love you and I miss you.

> *She speaks with wisdom,*
> *and faithful instruction is on her tongue.*
> *She watches over the affairs of her household*
> *and does not eat the bread of idleness.*
> *Her children arise and call her blessed.* Proverbs 31:26–28

CHAPTER 28

Blue Ribbon Winner

Scott and Chris's adjustment back into public education was, for the most part, a smooth one:

"You have no standardized testing scores on your record for last year! Where did you go to school?" Chris's fifth grade teacher inquired of him the first week of school.

"In the jungle," Chris replied matter-of-factly.

"Oh!" she responded in surprise. "And who was your teacher?" she continued.

"My mother," he said.

"Just your mother?" her voice elevated a few notes in dismay. She scribbled a note to herself, "This child should probably be moved out of the gifted program—might even need to repeat fourth grade."

Fortunately, before anything drastic was done, the math and reading parts of the standardized test were administered and Chris scored in the ninety-fifth percentile. So much for repeating fourth grade.

Scott, a seventh grader, participated with a few of the other seventh grade students in the John Hopkins Talent Search. This involved taking the Scholastic Aptitude Test (SAT) in the first part of his seventh-grade year—tests not normally taken until the junior or senior year of high school. If the seventh grader is able to score above 650 in either the math or verbal section, he or she becomes eligible to attend a summer program for gifted youngsters at the John Hopkins University.

"I don't know why these kids waste their time on this test," the guidance counselor pessimistically complained. "No child in the history of this school has come anywhere close to those scores. And I don't think," she said, eying Scott, "that a child who spent his last academic year in the JUNGLE is likely to, either!" With such encouraging words, she dismissed Scott from her office with the registration form.

The scores came back in February. In the math section Scott's score was 670 and in the verbal section 680! His combined total was 1350, better than ninety-eight percent of all graduating seniors! The guidance counselor was dumbfounded, flabbergasted, perplexed, and astonished! "Apologetic" managed its way in there also.

Since I had been Scott's teacher the previous year, it made me look OUTSTANDING! But a few things need to be revealed about Scott.

When he was three years old, I had my first inkling of what was in store. We were visiting my sister in upper state New York. The "Word of Life" camp, at Schroon Lake, was putting on a production of "Revelations," so we decided to go.

It was an inspired show, with massive angel choirs, formidable judgment seats, terrifying DESTRUCTION and TRIBULATION, and awesome GLORY. Smoke, screams, and horrific booms added to the effect. But Scott and Chris were most impressed by the final lowering of the New Jerusalem, adorned with lights and shiny gold paint. The entire cast joined their voices in singing, and Jesus, in His ultimate Glory, was revealed. It was quite a sight!

We returned to Dea's home quite late. I was exhausted and quickly got the boys tucked into bed, with prayers said, and hasty good-night kisses distributed. Chris was asleep before I reached the door. Scott would follow shortly, I presumed.

But half an hour later, the light by Scott's bed was still on. As I went to turn it off, I noticed he was intently studying my Bible.

"Scott, what are you doing still up?" I scolded.

"I found it, Mom!" he jubilantly shouted, oblivious to the irritation in my voice.

"Found what?" I said crossly. "It's late! You should be asleep!"

"I found what they were talking about in the play tonight!" With that statement, my three-year-old son began to flawlessly read Revelations 21:

> *Then I saw a new heaven and a new earth, for the first heaven and the first earth had passed away, and there was no longer any sea.*
>
> *I saw the Holy City, the new Jerusalem, coming down out of heaven from God, prepared as a bride beautifully dressed for her husband...*

Mom and Dea had entered the room, and were standing on either side of me. Scott continued to confidently read,

And I heard a loud voice from the throne saying, "Now the dwelling of God is with men, and he will live with them. They will be his people, and God himself will be with them and be their God."

Mom and Dea looked at each other and then at me. "Oh my!" they exclaimed.

So that was when I discovered my three-year-old could read.

He entered first grade at the normal age and time, but stayed in first grade for only two months. His achievement tests on entering placed him on a seventh grade reading level and a sixth grade math level. So—in November he was moved to second grade in the school's gifted program.

That wasn't really an ideal situation. Second graders don't like first graders to "invade their turf" and are relentless in driving that point home. And first graders, even if they do read better than second graders, are still, emotionally, first graders.

"Go back to first grade, first grade baby!" they taunted as they held the door shut against his entry. Scott excelled scholastically in the following grades but limped along socially. Honduras was a respite.

In seventh grade, his accomplishments did not end with winning the state and national John Hopkins Talent Search. He entered his science project, "Reshaping the airplane: a study in wingless flight," in his junior high school science fair. He won the first place trophy. In the state science fair at Stockton, New Jersey, he received the second place award in the engineering category. In the tri-state Delaware Valley Science Fair, where he competed against the sixth, seventh and eighth grade finalists from New Jersey, Pennsylvania, and Delaware, he placed first in the engineering category and was awarded the silver medal in the overall competition encompassing all categories. He was the only New Jersey child to win a medal, as well as being the youngest by two years. In recognition of this achievement, the Franklin Institute Museum placed his name in their Hall of Fame that year.

He also won an essay contest and received a trip to the Space Academy in Huntsville, Alabama. Stevens Institute granted Scott a scholarship to study college level calculus and computer FORTRAN during the summer months, with the option of starting as a full-time college student in the fall. I nixed the full-time college business! The

Naval Air Development Center in Pennsylvania offered him a mentorship in his chosen field of interest for three weeks.

On awards night in his junior high school, Scott was given the outstanding math and the outstanding science award.

WHEW! Pretty heady stuff for a twelve-year-old seventh grader.

His academic accomplishments continued to soar in eighth grade. He divided his time between eighth and ninth grade classes, and after December he was officially made a ninth grader. He entered his current research project, "The effects of main wing modifications on catastrophic aircraft spins," in the Monmouth County Science Symposium, sponsored by the United States Army. He was one of eight semi-finalists in the state chosen to present their science research papers at the state-level Science Symposium. His was awarded FIRST PLACE. He was the only thirteen year-old ever to win. Now he was to go on to the National Science Symposium in Huntsville, Alabama.

During this time, Scott managed to garnish a few additional points of recognition. At the Martin Luther King Science Fair he received the Corporate Industrial Award. At the Delaware Valley Science Fair he, again, placed first in the Engineering category. He was asked to speak at the Exxon Research and Development Center, in Abington, New Jersey, concerning aircraft spins, and was honored at a state banquet for outstanding science achievements. In the Junior Engineering Technical Society Contest he placed second in computer technology in the state of New Jersey. Added to this, he won the NASA outstanding Science Achievement Award, the United States Marines Science Achievement Award, the Yale Engineering Science Achievement Award, the Kodak Photography Award, and the New Jersey General Assembly Citation Award!

On May 16, he flew to Huntsville, Alabama, to participate in the National Science Symposium. He was so small, a special platform had to be placed behind the podium so that he could be seen as he delivered his paper. The auditorium was packed. Dignitaries and field experts were placed in seats of honor.

But somewhere in the large assemblage, Scott knew the most important person was sitting: his father! Cliff had come to see his son, and for Scott, the fact that his father was there made everything else pale in importance.

Scott confidently presented his paper and fielded the questions posed by the experts. He was interviewed and a half-page spread appeared about him in the New York Times. His next destination was to the International Science Symposium in London, England, where he would spend a "fortnight" and compete against the top Science students from thirty-three other countries. He was so young, special permission had to be sought for him to attend. He was only thirteen and the average age of the participants was nineteen. No one younger than sixteen had ever attended.

These achievements were incredible and a bit frightening for me as his mother. Scott just seemed to "go with the flow," unruffled and unaffected.

Before he left for London in July of 1990, Governor Florio, then Governor of New Jersey, asked Scott to meet with him in his office. Six armed guards were stationed around the room, connected with walkie-talkies. A delegation from the Middle East was leaving as we entered. Newspaper photographers were on hand to capture the moment Governor Florio shook Scott's hand to wish him the best in London, England. It was a genuine public relations event, a true "Kodak Moment!"

He spent ten fantastic days in London, visiting Oxford University, the London Tower, and he even got a quick glimpse of the Queen Mother passing by. While he was enjoying the sights, his paper was chosen for presentation in this very prestigious conclave of the best young minds in the world.

Not bad for a thirteen-year-old freshman who spent his previous year in the jungle!

> *All your sons will be taught by the* LORD,
> *and great will be your children's peace.*   Isaiah 54:13

PART III

Guatemala: I Will Know You, Lord

CHAPTER 29

Not Again, Lord!

While Scott's incredible achievements were mounting, other concerns were also swirling and bumping about. In November, Mission Aviation Fellowship had contacted me about returning to the mission field. Their need for teachers in Central America was still present and critical.

The same, unmistakable, finger of God, that had poked and prodded me before Honduras, was poking and prodding again. His gentle presence was calling me to trust Him once more.

"Hey, boys, how would you like to go back to Central America?" I posed, testing their reaction.

Without one moment's hesitation both boys shouted, "Yay! Great! When can we go?"

"Well, I guess I won't get any resistance from that direction," I surmised, a bit chagrined at the hope of an easy "out."

My reaction wasn't so spontaneous or so enthusiastic. All those hurdles that appeared one mile high before, now loomed two miles high!

I immediately started projecting my "demands." We couldn't go back to a place as remote as Ahuas, Honduras. Scott's academic needs were way beyond a one-room schoolhouse and me as his teacher. There would have to be high school facilities.

The Christian Academy of Guatemala was suggested. It was a mission school in Guatemala City covering kindergarten through twelfth grade and serving more than forty different mission groups. They needed elementary and junior high teachers desperately.

"Okay," I thought. "That would probably do..."

Hey! I'd been down this path before. I saw God's hand of provision supply all my needs. I felt His intimate care and love. Hadn't I been paying attention? I should have leaped with confidence and joy at the opportunity to follow the Lord's leading. I should have boldly proclaimed from the start, "HERE AM I, LORD. SEND ME!"

No, I didn't do that. I sadly confess that I flunked my test on "Stalwart, Obedient Sainthood"—again. I started complaining to the Lord, just like I did before. "No, Lord, I can't do it again," I moaned in prayer. "Bug somebody else to go as a teacher," I sulked.

Every box that had to be packed, every church that had to be visited, every letter that had to be written, every uncertainty that had to be placed in God's hand stood as an insurmountable barrier. Even my internal thoughts began to battle God's sovereignty. "Maybe," I rationalized, "I am doing this myself. Maybe I am only imagining that God wants me to go. Maybe this isn't really His will for me after all." But God's Presence would not let me feel peace when I tried to turn my back on His leading.

A new deterrent had been added to the mix. Scott's incredible academic achievements brought a chorus of objections from friends, family, and acquaintances, to any plan of leaving the United States school system. "Think," I was told, "of the harm you will do him. He needs special educational considerations. His gift needs to be fostered and nurtured. How can you do that in a third world environment?" It was true that plans were already in motion at his high school for a custom curriculum. A scholarship to an elite private school was a possibility.

This all sounded logical and a pretty good objection to bring before the Lord.

"Lord," I addressed, "I can't go to Guatemala. I have to think about Scott's schooling. I have to make sure he gets the best education." This was a reasonable consideration, I speculated, and one God would have to understand.

"Child," His quiet Presence responded to my self-important prayer. "Child, who is it that gave your son his intelligence? Who is it that blessed him with his abilities?"

"Lord, you did," I had to humbly concede.

"Yes, and if I am the one who gave him his abilities, I have prepared a use for them. And if I have a purpose and a use for them, surely, I will mold his talents and intellect to achieve that purpose. Trust me, child. I will watch over your son's education and provide him with exactly what he needs."

Yes, God was in control. I positively could not take credit for Scott's gift. There again, was that element of *Trust,* the tenet I kept stumbling over every time.

172

As much as Scott's academic achievements were mind-boggling, his social abilities were not keeping pace. The more he was pushed ahead in grade, the less he had in common with other kids. How could he? He was a thirteen-year-old among fifteen- and sixteen-year-olds. They were into dating and parties. He still needed to be convinced that girls didn't have cooties. I watched him become more and more absorbed with his computer and intellectual pursuits, and less and less involved with people around him. This concerned me. As smart as he was, he still needed to learn to live in the world around him. But how would going to Guatemala help him?

"Trust me." God would whisper. "Trust me. Have I ever let you down? Trust me. I will watch over you now, and always."

I took the first, hesitant step to follow the Lord to Guatemala. A leave of absence was requested, again, from my school. It was granted. I asked Cliff if he would give permission for the boys to leave the country, again. It was granted. I went to my pastor to seek prayer and monetary support. It was granted. Churches were visited and letters were written. Support was received. The boxes were packed. The supplies were bought. The only matter left was the renting of my house. This didn't happen until a week before we were to leave—just another issue of trust. But it did get rented. Should I have doubted?

Chris and I left for Guatemala City the beginning of August, 1990. Scott didn't travel with us because he was at the International Science Symposium in London, England. But after the "fortnight" he didn't return to the United States, but instead, he met us in the third world country of Guatemala, void of educational acceleration, void of prestigious science competitions or elite private schools, void of the glory and honor he was acquiring. But full of the love and guidance of his heavenly Father. "Trust me, my child, and see if I don't accomplish all that I set out for you. Trust me!" God's admonition reverberated through the pages of my Bible.

Trust!

I will instruct you and teach you
in the way you should go;
I will counsel you and watch over you.
Do not be like the horse or the mule,
which have no understanding

but must be controlled by bit and bridle
*   or they will not come to you.*
Many are the woes of the wicked,
*   but the* LORD*'s unfailing love*
*   surrounds the man who trusts in him.*
Rejoice in the LORD *and be glad....*   Psalm 32:8–11

CHAPTER 30

Buses, Bombs, and Bandidos: ¡Bienvenido!

Honduras exists in my memory colored in drab browns, olives, and grays; layered between heat, mildew, and bugs. Guatemala, in contrast, was vibrantly alive: dancing in reds, oranges, and yellows, the cool mountain air scented by Gardenia blossoms. The elevation of Guatemala City was about 5,000 feet above sea level, high enough to be above the stifling tropical heat, and high enough to give me an instantaneous nose bleed upon arrival.

Our house was spacious by anyone's standard. There were four bedrooms, a kitchen, dining room, living room and a maid's quarters—something none of my previous homes would have even dared dream of possessing. The concrete walls echoed hollowly as we moved about in the rooms. There was a fireplace and a small courtyard, where giant poinsettias bowed majestically in the breeze and colorful impatiens skirted the perimeter.

The one incongruous element to this picture was the eight-foot spiked fence that surrounded the house—oh, and also the barred windows and the front door with multiple locks, an inside security bar, and gouge marks by the latch where previous attempts were made at uninvited entry.

The school I would be teaching in was conveniently located right across the street. The small campus consisted of a house, two concrete out-buildings, and a wooden barn-like structure where gym and chapel took place. The Christian Academy of Guatemala provided education for almost 100 children from kindergarten to twelfth grade. There was a library, a multipurpose area, and a room for "field educated children." These were children whose remote location made it impossible for them to attend regularly, but who came in for a week or so every month or two. Families from thirty to forty different mission groups sent their children to the Academy. Mennonite, Southern Baptist, Pentecostal, and Lutherans; pilots, doctors, Bible translators, preachers, radio broadcasters, and computer specialists were all represented.

Our adjustment was a lot less traumatic than in Honduras. There were no bug invasions, confiscated toilets, or bat attacks to contend with. I started off teaching seventh- and eighth-grade reading and English. Chris fit right in with the twelve other seventh graders. Thirteen-year-old Scott was now a tenth grader, fresh from his academic conquest in London. But such heady accomplishments did not have the same impressive weight here in Guatemala. He was just one of twenty-five other high school students that shared the same four classrooms, with the same four teachers. Science symposiums and accelerated courses were not even on the menu.

One initial obstacle I encountered was TRANSPORTATION. I was used to my own car, an Oldsmobile Cutlass Supreme, fully loaded, with plush upholstery, power windows, and an AM/FM stereo tape deck. Here, the only option was a public bus: a very old orange, yellow, red, green, purple and blue school bus, bedecked with pompoms, naked ladies, and religious icons, with an unlimited capacity for human cargo. When the bus was full, by my standards, people continued to crush in, pushing and shoving until I was plastered, cheek-to-cheek, eyeball-to-eyeball, with at least six total strangers. Passengers would hang from the windows, dangle from the door, and clutch the roof. The idea of a bus being TOO full was preposterous. There always was room for at least twenty more people.

We were traveling on one such bus to Antigua, a town thirty miles from the capital, with another family from school. We had the uncommon delight of actually sitting in seats. The road followed a treacherous stretch of mountainous terrain. It was a good thing we were traveling during the day: few buses had operating headlights. At night a young boy would hang out from the front door waving a flashlight up and down, supposedly to guide the bus through the steep mountain pass. Reliable brakes were also a hit-or-miss proposition on buses. Linda, my traveling companion, was intent on pointing out to me hundreds of small wooden crosses and flower arrangements along the road.

"Each cross marks where someone has died in an accident on this road," she explained. "When you see a whole bunch of crosses together, that's usually where a bus went off the road."

This bit of newsy information had a decidedly unsettling effect on me. The road was virtually lined with those irksome little crosses.

Suddenly, all the standing passengers, in unison, knelt down on their knees. I was totally shaken. I whispered hoarsely to Linda, "This must be a really dangerous place in the road. Maybe we should have a moment of prayer too."

She looked at me, a bit bewildered, and asked, "What makes you think that?"

"Why, didn't you see everyone get down on their knees and pray?" I responded. By now everyone was back up on their feet.

She looked around and then began to laugh. "Cyndy, they weren't praying. We just passed a military check-point and the bus isn't supposed to have standing passengers. Didn't you see the bus driver motion for everyone to squat so it looked like we all had seats? It wasn't a dangerous stretch of road. He just didn't want his bus stopped for overcrowding."

Overcrowding! Like that was some nonexistent state of affairs in Guatemala! On future bus trips I also squatted in "prayer" past many a check-point.

After seven months of public transportation, God blessed me with a car: a fifteen-year-old, manual transmission, four-passenger, four-door Datsun. I have never appreciated anything more than that dull, soot gray, beat-up and dented old car! The back lights didn't work, and only one front light operated. There was a large hole in the floor board by the driver. I joked that it helped when the car needed a "running start" in the morning. But it also made me maneuver large puddles very carefully. And there was a novel addition of a toilet paper roll dispenser under the glove compartment. I had already learned such necessities of civilized life were not to be taken for granted. Either you carried your own supply or pay five centavos a sheet to the bathroom matron and that was only in the better locations. The boys discovered why God placed so many trees in Guatemala.

Guatemala was notorious for car thefts. One women I knew had her car taken from her as the man held a knife under her chin. But my Datsun was so beat up and ugly I could park it in the center of Guatemala City, unlocked, and come back an hour later to find a note saying, *"No, gracias. No lo queremos,"*—we don't want it! This didn't really happen but we did come back to a street where five cars had been ripped off and ours was the only one left.

In spite of its woe-begone appearance that car had an engine that could outlast the Duracell Bunny and the Timex watch combined. It surely "took a lick'n and kept right on tick'n"—and clank'n, puff'n and rattle'n down the road. It took us to the Pacific Ocean, ancient Mayan ruins, the base of an active volcano (we climbed to the peak on foot), and anywhere else it was pointed.

If we passed someone we knew, we adopted the Guatemalan custom of always stopping to give him or her a lift, even if we already had seven or eight people in the car. Chris would sit, straddling the gear shift console, two people would squeeze in the passenger seat, and Scott along with four others would fit in the back seat. Occasionally the trunk held a passenger or two as well. Room was so cramped I couldn't shift, so Chris pitched in for me. "Shift to first, now second! Third! Go back to first—now second! Third!" I barked as we tootled along. Chris got quite proficient at shifting with his LEFT hand, something, I warned him, that might cause problems when he learned to drive later on.

Police road blocks were a real hazard, especially if you were a blond-haired American woman traveling alone. The road blocks were for the sole purpose of extracting money from the easiest prey they spotted. The police would pick me out from a stream of traffic and wave me over to the side of the road. Then would proceed to find something wrong with my car or license, both areas of fertile opportunities. A threat was made to impound my car (this always happened when I was at the maximum distance from my home) and only an expected GENEROUS bribe could induce the relinquishing of my car. The money had to be passed to the policeman in a prescribed manner, slid up the inside of the door out of sight until it brushed his hand, which would be resting on the window. He would catch it between his fingers and if the amount agreed with him I was a free person again. If it didn't, then the maneuver was repeated once more.

After feeling like I was single-handedly supporting the Guatemalan fiscal budget, I started to pretend to be looking the other way when I saw a policeman begin to motion with his hand. Few Guatemalan police had cars so how would he catch me, I figured. After all, if I didn't "see" him motion to me, I wasn't really doing anything wrong if I just kept driving on past. But just to be on the safe side, I told Scott to peek out the back window and if he saw the policeman pull out his gun, I WOULD STOP!

No gun was ever pulled out. I just became one less victim in the scheme for getting rich under the table—or maybe that's "under the car."

Life was dangerous in Guatemala. The guerrillas were still waging war with the government and with everyone else for that matter. We frequently would have no electricity because an electrical tower or power station had been bombed. One day as we were shopping in an open-air market near our home, a large BOOM shook the pavement we were standing on. Billow of black smoke arose from the next block. Apparently a judge living there had been a target.

And *bandidos* were rampant. You could not walk safely down a street if you were wearing any sort of gold jewelry or designer sunglasses. I forgot this one day as I was browsing in the Central Market. I was still wearing my gold necklace, the last present Cliff had given me. A man approached, glaring at me as he neared. I was aware of him but not prepared for the speed in which he snatched my necklace and yanked it from my neck. He was off, running down the street before the whole incident registered in my brain. Both boys were beside me and hadn't even noticed him! Oh well, I shrugged. That was the last piece of gold jewelry I had to worry about anyway. I just felt fortunate I wasn't wearing gold earrings!

Our house was broken into also. We had left for school at seven thirty, as usual. And, as usual, I had instructed our small Miniature Schnauzer, Brittany, to guard the house. Brittany weighed ten pounds and had the courage of a mouse.

But she did have a shrill yip that echoed unmercifully in the concrete rooms.

Shortly after we left, a man, arriving on a bicycle, scaled our eight-foot spiked fence and entered our house with the help of a crowbar. The only room that contained anything of value was the upstairs guest room. There we kept the television set and Scott's computer. Some money had been casually left on the bed the previous night. For no particular reason, Chris had closed the door to that room that morning.

An hour after we had arrived at school, the maid next door called to tell me that Brittany would not stop barking, and when she went to investigate, she saw a man running out of my house, jump over the fence and make his get-away on a rusty old bicycle. She advised I come home immediately.

Scott, Chris and I arrived moments later. The front door was wide open. Everything in the downstairs rooms was in total disarray. Drawers were tossed about, furniture moved. The upstairs rooms were no

179

better. All my clothing from my drawers had been thrown around, the boys' things scattered. But we could find nothing missing. We possessed no expensive items of worth, and had no large sums of money stashed away—the things he was obviously in search of. And then we noticed the door to the guest room was still closed. "Oh no!" I exclaimed. "The computer and television set! Those are probably the things he was looking for!" I shouted. We bolted into the room to find—it had not even been touched. The money was still lying casually on the bed. The computer and TV were still there. Nothing had been moved. The robber had totally bypassed that area.

Had he even noticed the room? Had God averted his vision? Had Brittany's barking unnerved him? He had spent considerable time in our house but left with nothing. This was something that just didn't happen in Guatemala. We hailed Brittany, timid Brittany, as the hero, saying her barking had scared the big, bad, *bandido* away. But if she really had, the truth is, she was probably barking from under a bed.

I think I'll give the credit to God above. His hand had been over our house in New Jersey once before when a small boy was afraid. It was now resting securely on our home in Guatemala. Thank you, God.

> *But I trust in you, O* LORD;
>   *I say, "You are my God."*
> *My times are in your hands; ...*
> *How great is your goodness,*
>   *which you have stored up for those who fear you*
> *which you bestow in the sight of men*
>   *on those who take refuge in you.*
> *In the shelter of your presence you hide them.*

Psalm 31:14–15,19–20

CHAPTER 31

In the Presence of Evil

Cakchiquel, Quiché, Pokomchí, Kekchi, Mame, Tzutuhil: the Indians of Guatemala, each a unique people, each separated by their distinctive clothing and their particular language—but all tangled together by the complicated web of Mayan paganism, superstition, and Spanish Catholicism. These Indian natives gave Guatemala its vibrancy and color; its customs, traditions and holidays.

I was standing in a graveyard on a warm October morning. The sky was a brilliant blue. Young boys and men were running wildly about me, jumping over dirt mounds and screaming ecstatically as their giant circular kites would begin to take flight, or moaning inconsolably if they fell. The kites were forty to sixty feet in diameter, decorated with bright colorful designs. The launching of each kite was a complicated affair that took a crew of at least ten people. They were beautiful to watch, a giant kaleidoscope of colored disks bobbing in the hemisphere.

But this was a not a fun lark on a Saturday afternoon. These men were intensely serious in their endeavor. It was All Saints Day, the Day of the Dead, the day the dead demanded to be remembered properly—or else their spirits would come back and cause the families of these men harm. Each kite contained a message to the deceased relatives of a family. It was believed that the first kite to attain flight guaranteed that the dead ones would receive the message and all would be well for that family in the coming year. But a kite that did not ascend was a sign of misfortune.

The women had decorated the graveyard with colored streamers. Each mausoleum was draped in a mass of garlands, and each grave mound strewn with flowers. A bounteous smorgasbord of food had been placed at the foot of each grave with the hope that the dead relative would find the food pleasing and would eat it during the night. Amazingly, the food was always gone the next morning—and smug expressions had appeared on the local dogs overnight!

If the dead were remembered properly their spirits would bless the home and the corn crop would grow well. But if the spirits were not pleased, if they did not like the food offered, or if they did not receive a message on a kite, they would cause harm and destruction.

Good and evil, beauty and ugliness, ecstasy and fear, fortune and destruction: all mingled together in the life of a Guatemalan Indian. The capricious gods of their people existed all around them and had to be appeased continually. Jesus was seen as only one of a large cast of deities. He was called the "White Man's God." There was also *Jefe Dios,* Boss God. The saints that lined the walls of the Catholic church had names interchangeable with those of Mayan wood and field deities. Each saint was fed and clothed, paraded and entertained, to seek special favors.

In November we traveled to Chichicastanago for market day. All the wares and finery of the local Indians were on display. We were thoroughly enjoying the local sights as we ambled up and down the narrow village streets.

"Mom, what is that man doing?" Scott inquired as we approached the town plaza. On the steps of the church, a man appeared to be waving a dead chicken over his head. People were kneeling down in front of him as he sprinkled the chicken's blood on them. Lit candles cascaded down the steps.

I didn't know what to say to Scott. I sure didn't know what to make of it either. But a friend we had met in town overheard his question and explained, "He's a shaman, a witch doctor. Each person must go to the witch doctor first before entering the church. He prays for them and asks permission from the spirits for their entry. Without their permission, bad luck and misfortune would fall upon them."

That was a sobering clarification. Common sense said I probably should not enter this church but curiosity propelled me forward. Under the Blood of Jesus Christ we entered the side door of the church. The inside was dark and malevolent. The statues of the saints/gods were in their respective niches along the wall. At the altar was a large, glass casket with the most gruesome representation of Jesus in it I had ever seen in my life! The form was lying down. It was gaunt and tortured, with the eyes of a mad man, and blood covering its arms, legs, and protruding ribs. The appearance of this icon was positively frightening.

An old Indian woman had been kneeling in front of this sepulcher and quickly got up when she saw us. She lit a candle, then pulled a bottle of liquor from her bag and entered a dark chamber to the side of the altar.

"Where is she going?" I asked my friend in a whisper.

"She's going to make an offering to the evil one now," was the reply.

"What do you mean?" I asked, feeling a chill go down my spine. "There is a room for the evil one right here in this church?!" I gasped, incredulous.

"Yes. Not all churches have one—but this one does. After all, what good does it do, they feel, to appease only the good God? The bad god could get jealous and still cause mischief. So they appease the good god first with candles and money. Then they go into that dark room, where there is a wooden statue of the evil one, and they appease him with liquor and cigarettes. That way they are covered from both sides."

My heart broke for these people enslaved in a religion of fear and superstition. The evil one was a prominent being throughout Guatemala. In Santiago Atitlán, where we had gone with an evangelical puppet team, little boys followed us through the streets whispering "Maximon... Maximon...."

"Why are they saying that?" I asked, unnerved by their persistence.

"That is the name of the evil one. They are asking if you want to be taken to his house. They get money from tourists for leading them to Maximon's house," Jeanette answered. She was one of the Wycliffe missionaries, and pronounced the *x* in "Maximon" with a *sh* sound.

"He has a house?" I asked, apprehensively.

"The location is supposed to be a secret, but the local Indians take good care of him. They clothe him in silk scarves and provide him with ample cigarettes and liquor. This area is well known for its worship of Maximon and the shamans are very powerful because of it," Jeanette continued.

That was the truth. The shamans were powerful figures, and not just in this village. They fanned the fires of superstition and kept the people bound to these heartless deities. It was also believed that they held in their hands the ability to bless or curse a man's life. It was to a shaman a man would go if he wanted to seek revenge on his enemy. For a price, a few pieces of clothing, and a snippet of hair, an enemy's stomach could be filled with frogs, his strength sapped, and his spirit sent to wander.

On our route to school, we passed a tree of no particular interest until one day, we noticed a man's pants tied to its trunk. At first the legs were normally aligned but after a few days they began to take contorted positions. A few days later a shirt was added, its arms twisted oddly. A few weeks later a scarf appeared, tied as a noose, and then a sock with nails in it, a belt drawn too tight, and some hair. The form on the tree was growing grotesque and each new item bent unnaturally.

I didn't know who the victim of this hex was or what ill effects he was feeling, but everyday I would pray for him, for his protection and salvation. For three months the effigy had grown on the tree. For three months I prayed for this man. Then one day, it just vanished. Every bit of clothing, hat, shirt, shoes and belt were gone. It is a story I have no ending for. Did the victim discover this tree and take the things down? Did he die or was he saved? Did the curse just not work and the perpetrator remove it? Or did he run out of money to pay the shaman? I only have one sure answer. The God I was praying to is far stronger and more caring than any idol made of wood. The prayers I bathed him in each day had the blood of the Savior and the tears of His love. There is no bondage made by man that the Savior cannot break. On this fact I will rest all eternity.

The year was passing quickly. Christmas came and went in an explosion of fire crackers and with ample servings of *tamales*. The New Year was ushered in with a similar crescendo of exploding rockets. Now spring was here, although in this "land of eternal spring" the trees betrayed no change. *Semana Santa,* the Holy Week, had arrived. The streets of every village, town and city were decorated with large, floral *alfombras*: intricately patterned sawdust rugs in the vibrant reds, purples, yellows, and oranges of Guatemala.

Work on these *alfombras* had been nonstop, day and night, since Monday of Holy Week. The creation had to be finished by Good Friday, the day of the holy procession. A large platform with a statue of Jesus carrying His cross would be solemnly paraded through the streets of each village. Fifty or more men had paid the church for the privilege to bear the weight of the heavy platform on their shoulders. Hundreds more followed on either side as the procession wound up and down the streets and over the *alfombras,* whose creators believed they would receive penance as the platform passed over. Smaller platforms carrying Mary, the disciples, and the various saints completed the procession and hundreds of people lined the thoroughfares seeking favors and absolution as the statues passed them.

The day was a flurry of color, activity, and pageantry. But when Easter Sunday came, the day of Christ's resurrection and victory over death, the streets were quiet and deserted. There were no Catholic masses, no parades, no ringing of bells, no joyous celebrations for the greatest day of celestial victory in all Christiandom. The day went by without a notice.

As I gazed at the crucifix hanging on the door of the Catholic church and the empty streets, I knew why God sent His servants to Guatemala. The Catholic church was three days short of the truth when the early *padres* presented the Christian message. They stopped on the day of pain and sorrow, but did not move forward to look inside the empty tomb. The cross they worship still has Christ on it. They did not realize the power of the victorious message on the empty cross, the cross of the risen Savior.

Christ HAS risen! He is triumphant. He has beaten death and suffering and the hold of the evil one. There is no fear in His love. And this is the message the missionaries today bring to the people.

He is more than the "white man's god." No other penance is needed to go before Him but a heart that seeks forgiveness.

1 Peter 5:7 says, "Cast all your anxiety on him because he cares for you." A Quiché man read a translation of this in his own language that said simply, "What matters to you, matters to Him." He looked at those words and then at the wooden statues about him. Tears came to his eyes with the awesome realization that this God, who ruled the universe and created the mountains, cared about him. This was not a capricious and spiteful being, inanimate and unfeeling as the wooden statues were. This God cared about him personally, loved him, and died on the cross to rise again, victorious for him, over death and sin and the evil one. The bondage to superstition and fear were broken for that Quiché man that day, as he knelt down before the risen Lord, Jesus Christ, and prayed.

This was the message the evangelical Christian world was bringing to Guatemala, and the message was being heard. Nowhere in the world was the church of Christ growing quicker or more dynamically than in Guatemala, for the truth had truly set them free! The shamans, Maximon, cursings, and fear had all been defeated at the foot of the empty cross. He is risen, and with Him there is victory and salvation.

For everyone born of God overcomes the world. This is the victory that has overcome the world, even our faith.

... The one who is born of God keeps him safe, and the evil one cannot harm him.   1 John 5:4,18

"Death has been swallowed up in victory."

"Where, O death, is your victory?
Where, O death, is your sting?"

... But thanks be to God! He gives us the victory through our Lord Jesus Christ.   1 Corinthians 15:54–57

CHAPTER 32

With Thanksgiving

At the end of the first year in Guatemala, we unanimously decided to stay another year. Both Chris and Scott liked the friends they had made, the school, and the adventure of living in another culture.

The third grade class I was teaching was fantastic. They were bright, inquisitive, and tender to the word of God. Not a behavior problem in the lot of them. If I were to dream up an ideal class in an ideal surrounding to teach, this would have been the class. And the parents were just as fantastic, both supportive and congenial.

It wasn't a difficult matter to stay another year. I had been on a year's leave of absence from my district, so a call was placed to the principal of my building, and to the superintendent, to request an extension on the leave. That was denied. But, it was explained, if I resigned I would not have to worry about getting my job back. I had an excellent reputation, had been nominated as the outstanding teacher of the year twice, and was well regarded by both the principal and the superintendent. Both of them gave me an oral promise that I would definitely be rehired once I came back to the States. I resigned without too much concern.

Year two began in Guatemala. The new third grade class was just as fantastic. My grasp of Spanish was a bit better. Our car was still chugging along. And both boys were now fluent in Spanish and developing into fine young men. Being on the mission field, I reflected, was truly an intimate experience with God. Stripped of the material luxuries and securities the United States offers, my dependence on Him was far greater and His presence so much closer.

August, September, and part of October slipped by. Letters from my sister kept me abreast of how things were going in New Jersey. She was in charge of collecting the rent payments from my tenants, depositing it into my checking account, and paying the mortgage and utility bills. All seemed to be going well. "However," she said, "there has been some difficulty getting the rent checks from the new tenants that moved in in August. Their checks keep bouncing. They are two months behind in the rent."

Two months became three months, and three months became four months. The tenants were obviously not paying their rent. They had decided that an "absentee landlord" meant a free ride for them. The bills and mortgage payments still had to be paid and the reserves in my savings account were getting lower and lower. Four months became five months—finally Dea was able to get them to leave. But new tenants needed to be found before money would come in again. The sixth mortgage payment was due and there was absolutely no more money left in my savings account, or in any other account, for that matter. I had no way of meeting the amount due and the possibility of losing my house became frighteningly real. Anxiety grabbed hold of every facet of my life.

It so happened that the class memory verse that week was Philippians 4:6–7:

> *Do not be anxious about anything, but in everything, by prayer and petition, with thanksgiving, present your requests to God. And the Peace of God, which transcends all understanding, will guard your hearts and minds in Christ Jesus.*

As I read the verse to the children, a feeling of complete futility and hopelessness swept over me. My anxiety, like a vise, constricted me. I had been presenting my petition to God, pleading with Him for help. But still no money had come or new tenants found. How could I give thanksgiving in this matter? I was about to lose my house!

"I can't teach you this verse, children," I apologized. Tears fought to well in my eyes. "I am very anxious right now because I have no money to pay the mortgage payments and I am about to lose my house. I do not know how to pray with thanksgiving about this," I confessed, my voice trembling.

The children received my statement with gravity and concern, and their young faces met mine with compassion. There was not a sound in the room for several minutes. Then a solitary hand raised in the air.

"Yes, Greg?" I questioned.

"You can thank Him for all the years you have lived in the house," Greg said shyly.

In the simplicity of his statement, all the memories, all the joys, all the fun, and all the warmth that house had provided flooded my mind.

Yes, I was thankful for all the years I had lived in that house, for the way God had provided that house, and the way He made it grow. Yes, He definitely had provided that house. I had gotten the mortgage for it in one day, even though I was newly divorced, without a credit rating, and without a job. That, in itself, was a miracle. I needed a house and He had provided. Would He not do it again?

"Yes, Greg," I said, smiling, though hardly able to seem him in my misted vision. "Yes, Greg, I can thank Him for all the years He has allowed me to live in that house. You are right! And you know what? I don't have to be anxious either, because He gave me that house, and He can do it again!"

As the full realization of this took possession, the peace of God, which truly transcends understanding fell upon me. Easily and effort-lessly a prayer of thanksgiving was sent to God. "Thank you, Lord, thank you."

That week I received three support checks that were double their usual amount.

One had a note attached that said, "For extra needs." There was no way they could have known how desperate my "extra need" was.

A week later, two mothers met me at the door of my classroom as I was dismissing the children. They handed me a plain, white envelope.

"Open it," they encouraged. "Open it."

The envelope was stuffed full, and I couldn't fathom what was inside. I tore the edge, looking for a letter or a child's artwork. Instead, lots and lots of green money poked out from the tear.

"What is this?" I asked in astonishment.

"It's for your mortgage payment," one mother explained. "The children told us about your house and each parent wanted to give what they could to help you. I hope it's enough."

Enough? How wonderful God is. He's a healer, provider, re-deemer, AND a mathematician. The money in the envelope and the three extra support checks came to EXACTLY the amount I needed for the payment!

The following day the phone rang.

"Hi, Cyndy," my sister cheerfully greeted me. "I have good news for you. The house has been rented and you have new tenants that are going to move in in a week."

Do not be anxious about anything. . .

CHAPTER 33

The Widow's Mite

It didn't take one with acute perception to notice that the standard of living varied widely between mission groups. Some were "tent makers" and survived on what they earned from a trade in Guatemala. Others lived modestly from month to month on what supporters sent. And others were supported by large mission boards with deep pockets. At times it was hard to justify the opulence displayed by these groups.

"Mom, did you see Nate's brother's new car?" Chris questioned excitedly one day after school.

"Yes, Chris, it's a beauty," I smiled, visualizing the red, sporty convertible the boy had driven to school in that morning.

"Nate said his parents spent a ton of money on that car!"

"I don't doubt it," I concurred, thinking back that any car, even a clunker, would cost twice as much in Guatemala as it would in the States.

"Mom, why can't we get a car like that?" he challenged.

"That's easy, Chris. Because I haven't got the money for a car like that. But even if I did, would it be right for me to buy a snazzy red sports car for one of my kids to drive in, with God's money?" I questioned him.

"Why not? I mean, if God gave you the money, why not?"

"Chris, do you remember the people who support us?"

"Yes," he said as he listed off relatives and people from our church. "What has that got to do with anything?"

"You forgot Mrs. Wiseman," I reminded him.

"Mrs. Wiseman? But she doesn't send us very much," he defended.

"That's just the point, though, Chris," I chided.

The story of Loretta Wiseman was a familiar one to him. She was a small, elderly lady, one of the first we had met when we started attending the Community Church. She had been the boys' Sunday school teacher when they were three and four years old. I think she had been EVERYONE'S Sunday school teacher when they had been three and four years old! No one could come close to matching the number of years she spent teaching young children about God's love. It was rumored that she had been a Sunday school teacher since the flood—but I didn't believe that one!

Sam, her husband, was a strong, powerful man, powerful in stature and powerful in the Lord. He was the guiding hand of wisdom in the church. Even the pastor relied on him and his steady faith.

But he became sick and bone cancer whittled away his powerful frame. Loretta stayed by his side as even the strongest medication could not give him relief from the tormenting, searing pain. He cried to God for relief and was bewildered by the void. Pain trapped him cruelly in a prayer-less prison. Loretta held his hand and prayed.

She prayed when he couldn't. She prayed when her heart broke seeing the agony he was in. She prayed when he screamed at God, "Why don't you love me any more?!" She prayed when he cried in her arms. And she prayed, with tears in her own eyes, when he finally was released and went home to his Lord.

After Sam passed away there was little left for Loretta to live on. But that was okay, she had said. God would take care of her needs. Whatever she had was the Lord's anyway, she acknowledged. Her house needed painting, the yard was overgrown, food was not plentiful, and the heat was turned too low. But with a sweater around her shoulders, she never failed to meet with the Lord each day and pray for the needs of others.

When I made my appeal for support as we prepared to go to Guatemala, many of the church families generously pledged—some twenty-five dollars, some fifty, and a few even a hundred dollars a month. As I was leaving the church, Loretta quietly handed me an envelope. In it was ten dollars and a note saying she would send ten dollars more each month.

"But, Loretta," I argued, "are you sure you can afford this?" She had so little to live on as it was.

She nodded and smiled. "I want to be a part of the Lord's work," she said. And every month a ten dollar bill was faithfully sent.

"Chris," I addressed him again. "There are many people who send us money. Some can afford to do it more easily than others, but I don't think anyone sacrifices more to do so than Mrs. Wiseman. But she does it because she wants to be a part of God's work. What if I wrote her a letter and said,

'Thanks, Mrs. Wiseman. We put the money you sent us for God's work towards a shiny, new convertible. We look really snazzy in it. Thanks for the sacrifices you have made!'

"Do you think that would be something that would honor her, or honor God?"

"No, Mom," Chris admitted. "I guess I had forgotten about her because she didn't send as much as the other people."

"But we are more accountable to Mrs. Wiseman than to anyone else on that list. And I praise God for her faithfulness."

> *This poor widow has put in more than all the others. All these people gave their gifts out of their wealth: but she out of her poverty put in all she had to live on.*   Luke 21:4

CHAPTER 34

Earthquake!

I don't handle earthquakes well. Some people can discover this fact while staying in their own backyards. It took me a 5,000-mile jaunt to Central America. Most times I am a sane and predictable person, but when the floor under my feet turns to jello, I lose all sense of rationality.

Guatemala is rife with evidence of earth tremors. Faults can be seen in road beds, walls, and excavations. Stories of previous quakes were rampant. But so far I hadn't experienced any personally. We were cautioned numerous times that if an earthquake were to strike, the best places to go were under desks, beds, tables, or door lintels—but NOT to run outside.

The house we lived in had two exits. One was at the far end of the house through a metal door in the laundry room. The other went out under a carport, which consisted of a heavy concrete slab held up by four slender, brick pillars. If there were an earthquake, it wouldn't take much to make that slab come tumbling down. But so far: no earthquakes, no problem!

In September, Mrs. Eastman came to stay with us for a short time. She was an elderly missionary woman from California. In spite of her age, she was one spry feisty little lady, convinced that God was not ready to "put her out to pasture yet." She had the zeal to evangelize all the Latino World single-handedly! She set up camp in the downstairs bedroom, just off the laundry room.

Each school morning followed the same regimented routine. I would wake up first, at 6:30 in the morning. After dressing, I'd wake the boys and then go downstairs to prepare breakfast. Mrs. Eastman's alarm would wake her up at 7.

On one such morning I was already downstairs in the kitchen. Mrs. Eastman's alarm hadn't gone off yet. The boys were stirring but barely. I felt the room start to shake, slowly at first, as if a very heavy truck were moving down the street. Then the gyrations became more forceful. As they intensified the floor heaved under my feet. Dishes crashed, cabinets flew open. Everything that had been firm, turned to gelatin. Sheer panic took over.

I started screaming, feeling trapped and afraid. *"Get out! Get out! It's an earthquake! Scott, Chris, Mrs. Eastman, get out! Get out!"*

The whole time I was hollering, I was frantically trying to unlock the five bolts and latches on the door to the carport. The floor continued to sway drunkenly.

"Get out! Get out!" I sobbed. *"Scott, Chris, where are you?"* I was making no progress with the locks.

As suddenly as the shaking began, it stopped. My screaming and sobbing echoed in the still room. The floor stopped its convulsive lurching.

"Scott, Chris?" I whispered.

"We're okay, Mom. We're here, under the doorway," they replied.

Like a reset button being pushed, awareness returned. Scott and Chris were crouched under the wide door lintel, one of the safest parts of the house. Then I looked at the door I was trying to flee through. "What a stupid thing to do," I thought. "This would have put me right under the concrete carport. Dumb move!" I chided myself.

"Phew! That was a close call," I remarked to the boys. "Your old mom was trying to do a really stupid thing. You were smart to stay where—"

I hadn't finished the sentence when a second tremor hit.

"Scott! Chris! Get out! Get out! Mrs. Eastman! Mrs. Eastman! Get out! Get out!" I screeched over and over again.

The same door, that moments before I'd recognized as the gateway to a deathtrap, I was frantically trying to open again, clawing at the locks, screaming and crying as the floor tossed and vibrated.

"Scott, Chris, Mrs. Eastman! You have to get out! Hurry! Get out! Get out!" I repeated incoherently. *"Get out! Get out!"* My voice kept beat with the shaking of the walls until it was only my voice that was shaking.

The tremor had stopped. My surroundings clicked into focus. The door to the carport was in front of me, with one lock now unbolted. Broken dishes were everywhere. Scott and Chris were still huddled under the door lintel, looking at me in complete astonishment! They had just witnessed their usually-in-control mom do one heck of a Banshee war dance in the front entryway.

Mustering as much composure as I could retrieve under the circumstances, I smiled sweetly and remarked, "I'm glad you boys stayed under the doorway. That was the right thing to do."

Looking back at the door, I couldn't believe I was still trying to get out that way. The table, the desk, the doorway, all would have offered better protection. Why did I feel so strongly that I had to exit this way? How dumb can a person be? And where was Mrs. Eastman?

I started to call, "Mrs. East—"

The third tremor hit!

"Scott, Chris, Mrs. Eastman! Get out! Get out!" I was screaming and clawing at the front door all over again. Chains rattled, the wood reverberated. There was a crashing on the other side of the door! Still, I persistently attempted to escape. *"Scott, Chris, Mrs. Eastman! We have to get out!"*

This tremor only lasted a few seconds, long enough for me to add one final notch of hysteria to my Banshee War Whoop. I was crouching and jumping up and down alternately, banging on the wood panels, screaming, sobbing, and hiccuping.

"Mom, it's over," Scott called uncertainly. "It's over."

For the third time, consciousness returned. I stood up. The boys were safe. We all were safe. Dishes lay broken on the floor. Pictures hung askew. But where was Mrs. Eastman? I walked back to her room and knocked.

"Mary? Mrs. Eastman?" I called.

After a pause, a sleepy voice responded, "Is it time to get up? My alarm hasn't gone off yet."

I waited a minute before I answered.

"No, Mary," I conceded, "you have ten more minutes. I'm sorry I woke you."

CHAPTER 35

Falling Securities!

The end of the second year was approaching. Discussion began about what we needed to do to get ready to return to the States. Unexpected resistance came from Scott. He did *not* want to go back yet. He begged to finish out high school in Guatemala and graduate with his class here. It was not hard to understand why he wanted to do that but there were other matters to consider, such as being in a high school in the States so that he would be eligible for scholarships. As a single mom there was no way I was going to have the kind of money needed to send him to college, any college—and especially the really good college that his intellect seemed to need. No, he needed to be in a state-side high school where his academic achievements would make him noticed for scholarships.

It was May and time, I resolved, to make a call to my New Jersey school district and cash in on those two verbal promises that I would be rehired. With optimism I asked the operator to connect me to the states. The optimism didn't last long. The board office secretary informed me that the superintendent was no longer working in the district. He had accepted a job in a larger district. Promise number one just evaporated.

"Can I be connected with the principal of the elementary school, please?" I asked.

"She's out to lunch," the pleasant voiced woman said.

"She! Isn't...isn't the principal of that school a man?" I stammered.

"Oh no, not any more," the woman laughed. "He resigned around the first of the year. He's now superintendent in a school district up north."

"That can't be!" I gasped as promise number two just went "poof" and vanished. "Who is the new superintendent and who is the new principal?" I sputtered out.

I didn't recognize either of the names she gave me. Both were hired from outside the district and neither of them knew me. I hung up the phone in total dismay.

At this moment, the true, stalwart Christian saint would have immediately taken inventory of all the times and difficult situations God had already handled. This not-so-stalwart, nor-so-saintly, human being panicked and promptly took an inventory of all the ramifications of not having a job to go back to.

Another call, this one quite a bit more desperate, was made to the district. I would find SOMEONE who knew me! From one office to another my call was transferred until it landed in the office of the Director of Special Services. He remembered me! And—he was even willing to give me a job as a teacher in a neurologically impaired classroom.

"That's fantastic! Thank you!" I bubbled out. My next question concerned the salary.

"I don't have good news for you in that department," he stated pessimistically. "The board voted this year to change their policy concerning the hiring of teachers with experience. Since you resigned you would have to fall under their new guidelines. Let's see... Here it is," he said as he must have found a book to use as reference. "To determine where you are on the pay scale, every two years of experience would count as only one. How many years of experience do you have?" he asked.

"Sixteen," I said. I had added the twelve years of public school plus the three years in the mission schools, plus the year I would be starting. But in truth, I should have said "thirteen." The three years on the mission field in a "Christian" school would seldom be counted towards experience in a "public, secular" school.

"Sixteen would put you on the eighth level on the pay scale," he matter-of-factly stated.

That all too familiar feeling of panic, major panic took over. I had been on the thirteenth level when I left. Eighth level! If I had told the truth I would only be on the sixth level, less than half of what I was making when I left. I couldn't live on half my salary! I was pretty sure I couldn't live on three quarters of it either.

"Could you add in the three years of experience here in Central America?" I asked, fully aware they were already part of the number I had given him.

"Okay," he benevolently and generously agreed. "That brings your experience level up to nineteen," he said.

"What about the four years I taught in South Carolina?" I asked. That number was also in the original sixteen I had given him, but hey, he had just magically added three more years to my experience—why not try for more?

"Did we include that?" he asked.

"No," I blatantly lied! I was desperate to get the years of experience up to a level that I could live on.

"Okay, let's see. Nineteen plus four more brings it to twenty three. That would put you on the eleventh step.

Eleven wasn't thirteen, but it was a lot closer to it than the truthful level of SIX. Maybe if I really budgeted well, I could make ends meet, I contemplated. But it would be really, really tight—*really* tight!

"Okay," I agreed. "I'll take the job. Thank you. I really appreciate what you have done," I added. "Could you send me something to confirm you are rehiring me with twenty-three years of teaching experience?" I inquired daringly.

"I will send you a contract in the mail," he said. "The figure will be on your contract."

I hung up the phone marveling that I had just gained seven years of experience in only twenty-five minutes. Not bad! The easiest seven years of teaching in my life!

But the euphoria didn't last long, maybe all of five minutes. Crawling up the sides of my consciousness was incipient GUILT.

"You lied," a voice inside me taunted.

"I had to!" I rationalized. "I can't live on half my salary. It wouldn't even cover my mortgage payments."

"You lied," the voice continued to accuse.

"I have two children to support. I have to think of them."

"You lied."

"It wasn't fair of them to take away my years of experience! I earned those years! They are mine!"

"You lied."

"I can't take chances in this. It's too important! How is Scott going to get into college? He needs scholarships to pay for it, scholarships that I can't get here in Guatemala."

"You lied."

"I can't put my well-being and the well-being of my children at stake! I have nothing else to fall back on. I need money to live on, to pay the bills, and to feed my children! I need money for college tuition. God, you just have to understand!"

But the voice would not be quieted. "Who are you serving and who are you trusting?" it quietly posed.

"God, my trust can only go so far," I countered. "You let me down too. I left my job and family to follow you. I resigned, trusting you would keep my position safe for me. But you didn't! How can I live on a salary that's only peanuts compared to what it was. That wasn't supposed to be part of the package deal."

In an uncomfortable flash of insight, I realized at that moment that I had resigned, not trusting God to hold my job for me, but the promises of the two men and my good standing. And now I was putting my trust in the Director of Special Services to get my job back for me, at any cost.

It was hard to have a devotion time. My prayers would turn into arguments with God. My Bible stayed shut until church service on Sunday.

The pastor was speaking eloquently about a topic I was only half tuned in to. Internally, I was still trying to rationalize to God why it was okay to lie to get my job back. To make a point the pastor had the congregation turn to Jeremiah 17. I don't remember what we were directed to look at. My eyes fell on Jeremiah 17:5,7-8:

> *This is what the Lord says:*
> *"Cursed is the one who trusts in man,*
> *who depends on flesh for his strength*
> *and whose heart turns away from the Lord....*
> *But blessed is the man who trusts in the Lord,*
> *whose confidence is in Him.*
> *He will be like a tree planted by the water*
> *that sends out its roots by the stream."*

The words rang from the page with the force of a death sentence. I could not deceive myself. My trust was in man and not in God. Was I about to bring a curse down upon myself? What was I to do?

That night I opened my devotional book, *My Utmost For His Highest* by Oswald Chambers.

May 25: THE TEST OF SELF INTEREST

... God sometimes allows you to get into a place of testing where your own welfare would be the right and proper thing to consider if you were not living a life of faith.... Many of us do not go on spiritually because we prefer to choose what is right instead of relying on God to choose for us. We have to learn to walk according to the standard which has its eye on God. *"Walk before Me."*

God couldn't have spoken to me more clearly than if He pulled up an easy chair and sat down across from me. I couldn't go back to my old position on the basis of a lie. I knew that all along. I just didn't want to acknowledge it. To trust my own devices and the director's would be bringing a curse on my path. I had enough wisdom to know the lie would eventually be found out. And what reflection would that have on the God I served? Or on the fact that I called myself a missionary? I would have to let God choose my path, as uncertain and as unknown as it was. I had faced that uncertainty before but always with an earthly crutch to fall back on "in case God didn't come through." I always had a job to go back to, a salary I could depend on. But now there would be nothing—nothing but God to depend on.

"Lord, I'm sorry," I prayed humbly. "Please forgive me for not trusting you. How many times, Lord, must I stumble on trust? When will I learn that I can trust you no matter what?"

My hand shook as I dialed the phone the following day.

"Sir, I want to thank you so much for offering me the position. You have been there as a support for me so many times and I really appreciate it. I appreciate what you have done. But I have to decline the position at this time. Coming back at half my salary would be difficult and Scott wants to stay one more year to graduate with his class in Guatemala. Thank you, though, sir," I unpretentiously explained.

There was silence on the other end. Then, in an even-toned and controlled voice he pronounced, "You can expect never to have a job in this district again. You have put me in an awkward position. I already dismissed the teacher you would have replaced. That was unfair to her, and makes the excuse I gave her appear untrue. I trusted you to act more professionally. I wish you luck in whatever teaching position you secure when you return. Goodbye."

The dial tone rang hollow in my ear as I stood numb, still holding the phone. You can expect never to have a position in this district again! The finality of that statement shook me. But I deserved it. I had brought it upon myself. But now my last bit of self-preserving security had just been chopped off at the quick. Even at half salary I couldn't go back. There was absolutely nothing left to depend on but God.

Panic should have set in, but instead a strange peace settled over me. "Lord," I prayed, "all my props, crutches, monetary means, and earthly securities are gone. I have nothing but you. I am frightened when I look towards the future. I don't know how I will get a job when I go back, or where the money will come from that I need to pay the bills. I don't know how Scott will get into college or how I will pay for it. I don't know where Chris will go to high school. I don't even know where I will live, but it will all be worth it. It will be worth it if I positively know, at the end of this year, that you are who you say you are, *Jehovah Jireh,* God the provider... that in you there is no fear. That I can trust you NO MATTER WHAT. I want to trust you, Lord, and not always bolt at the first sign of trouble. Give to me a trust that is sure. Under your wing teach me to rest."

> *Trust in the Lord and do good;*
> *dwell in the land and enjoy safe pasture.*
> *Delight yourself in the Lord*
> *and he will give you the desires of your heart.*
> *Commit your way to the Lord;*
> *trust in him and he will do this:*
> *He will make your righteousness shine like the dawn,*
> *the justice of your cause like the noonday sun.*
> *Be still before the Lord and wait patiently for him;*
> *DO NOT FRET...*

Psalm 37:3–7

CHAPTER 36

All the World's a Stage

"Mom, Mr. Bendele says we need the costumes by next week. Can you have them ready?" both boys anxiously asked.

"Costumes?! Hey guys, this isn't a simple task of whipping together any old thing," I exploded. "Chris, you just need one, but Scott—you need five different outfits! This is really taxing my sewing skills—I don't have any patterns but you expect me to make appropriate clothes for the eighteenth century: breeches, waistcoats, shirts, and robes—and all by next week!" My anger was mixed with a healthy dose of anxiety.

The Academy was putting on a full-scale musical production entitled, "Ride, Ride," based on the life of John Wesley. It was to be performed in a large hall in the center of Guatemala City. Scott had the lead role of John Wesley, a man compelled to bring the message of "salvation by faith" to every man, even when barred from the pulpits of the Anglican Church. Chris was cast as a "lunatic," an appropriate contrast! The teacher behind the production, Paul Bendele, was a stickler for detail.

Paul had been at the Academy for three years, and Scott made an immediate attachment. The man was deeply committed to the Lord and theater was his medium of spiritual expression. He was a dynamo of energy, singularly focused on the goal of the moment, expecting nothing less than the same from each of the students in the cast. Rehearsals were long and late. Parts were repeated again and again, dance numbers and songs done over and over. His expectations seemed unreachable. And yet no teacher in Scott's life had a more profound influence than Paul Bendele.

Paul had put Scott in the lead role of the play. Scott was to convey every bit of the charisma of the man, John Wesley, from his youth to old age, while on stage. And Scott would rather have died a million deaths than disappoint Paul. In Paul's demanding style, he stretched Scott's abilities in music and technical skills. Hopping about the ladders, Scott looked like a small monkey as he changed electrical strings and mixed gels. Paul treated Scott as an equal, relying on him as his right-hand assistant and Scott loved every minute of the heightened intensity.

Scott's academic interests were put on hold. Interacting with people took priority. He stayed at school way past suppertime, helping Paul. At night he would study scripts or lighting charts or historical background. I was concerned about the demands Paul put on Scott, or maybe that Scott put on himself to get Mr. Bendele's approval.

"Scott?" I questioned in the dark. It was late and I saw light coming from Scott's room. Glancing at the clock, I angrily called again, "Scott, it's two-thirty in the morning! What are you doing still awake?!"

"Mr. Bendele wants me to write down the musical score for this song. He only has it on tape and he wants a score so that Mr. Minsky can play it on the piano," Scott apologetically explained.

"That's impossible!" I expressed with irritation. "How can he expect you to do such a thing? You don't have the musical experience!"

"But Mom, I've been working on it for quite a while and I think I almost have it," Scott explained. "He wants it for rehearsal tomorrow. Please Mom, I just have a little more to do," he begged.

"Was this what you were up late doing last night?" I probed.

There was a silence and then a hesitant, "Yes, Mom."

"And the night before that?"

A pause. "I guess so."

"Scott, it's so late—you'll never be able to function tomorrow. Turn off the light and I'll write him a note explaining you just weren't able to get it done for tomorrow's rehearsal," I said firmly.

"No, Mom! I have to have it finished. Please, just a few more minutes," Scott frantically pleaded.

Reluctantly I conceded. He said he was almost done so I expected his light would go off in a few minutes. I dozed back to sleep.

At five-thirty I woke with a start. Scott's light was still on. Furious, I stormed into his room: he was huddled over his desk, one small light fighting back the shadows, intently listening to a tape through earphones. Over and over he would play a section, checking what he had written, replaying, rechecking—then move to the next section. He looked up to see me standing in the doorway, hands on my hips and a scowl deeply drawn across my face.

"Mom, I'm done," he offered, appeasing. "I'm just checking to make sure it's right."

"Scott, it's five-thirty in the morning!" I hollered. "In an hour you have to get ready for school!"

"I know, Mom," he said quietly. "I'll be okay." There was a pause and then he added, "I did it! I got the score written down! I DID it, Mom!" An intense expression of achievement went out with that statement.

Two hours later we parted at the entrance of the school to go to our various classrooms. I didn't see Scott until late that night. When he walked in the door, his glistening eyes and the puffy redness betrayed that he'd been crying.

"Scott, honey, what's wrong?" I said with concern.

"Nothing, Mom," he attempted, but his voice choked with emotion.

"Scott, what happened?" I repeated gently.

"Oh, Mom!" his words flooded out. "You know the score I'd been working on for the past few weeks—I thought it was good. I really worked hard to get it just right."

"I know you did, Scott," I sympathized, waiting for the rest to come out.

"He didn't even try to play it," Scott moaned. "He just looked at it and said he couldn't use it. Just like that. He didn't even try it. All that work, and he's not going to use it." Scott slumped down on the staircase.

"He didn't say anything else to you?" I indignantly demanded, feeling my combat armor coming up in defense of my child. "He didn't say, 'Wow, I can see you put a lot of work in this!' Or, 'Thanks, Scott, for trying!' Anything?"

"No," Scott dejectedly whispered. "He just said he couldn't use it."

I have often compared myself to a she-lion when it came to my children. If anyone hurt one of them I was ready to do serious battle. And at this moment every one of my claws was out, ready for the attack. I didn't care that it was eleven at night.

Scott, always keen to my intentions, picked up his head as I headed for the phone. "Wait, Mom," he cautioned. "Don't call Mr. Bendele now. I can handle this. I'll handle it tomorrow."

"He doesn't have a right to take advantage of you like that!" I angrily stormed.

"Mom, just wait, okay?" he said. "Let me handle this."

I sat down beside him and held his hand as I prayed silently. First, in anger, I prayed for God's lightning bolts to come flashing out of the sky aimed at one particular person! But the anger was quieted in those still moments of prayer. The Holy Father's insight and wisdom took control of my errant words. How much I wanted to protect Scott from every hurt, sadness, and disappointment in life. But I couldn't do that. God uses joys and hurts to mold us into the image of His Son. Scott had long wanted the approval of his father, but his father was not there to give it to him. Now he desperately needed the approval of this man he looked up to and admired. But even the best of human beings slip at times. God doesn't want us to make idols out of humans. Respect is best seen through glasses of compassion and understanding.

"Scott. . ." He looked up, absorbed in his own misery. The calmness in my voice surprised both of us. "Maybe Mr. Bendele really didn't mean to be so curt. You know how much pressure he's under and the play is just about to open. I don't think he meant to put down your work. You did a great job, Scott, a really great job. There must be another reason. I know he still thinks a great deal of you. You didn't let him down, honey."

Tears welled in Scott's eyes again. "I tried so hard. . ."

"I know you did. Talk with him. You might find another side to his actions. Scott, no man is perfect. Even the best will let you down sometimes. Forgive him and pray for understanding."

The next day, so typically, was filled with classes, activities, meetings and rehearsals. My old self occasionally flared for control as I thought of Paul. It would have been so much easier to just go up to him and "knock his block off" with words of anger. But I was letting Scott deal with it, and allowing the Lord to use it for His purpose.

In the evening Scott and Chris returned from rehearsal exhausted. Chris went right off to bed. I caught Scott's arm as he was about to disappear also.

"Well?" I questioned, looking at him intently.

"Well what?" he so characteristically responded, evading the obvious inquiry.

"Well, did you handle it?" not letting him slip so easily from the question.

"Mom," he smiled. "Everything's okay. I told you not to worry. Mr. Bendele came up to me and apologized, even before I had a chance to say anything. He said that he realized last week that the number wasn't going to fit into the action. And even if it did, there wouldn't be time to perfect it with the chorus. He said he just forgot that I was still working on the score. You know how focused he is, Mom. He isn't perfect, but no one is." Those words sounded vaguely familiar from the night before. "But you know what? He's still the only one I know who could accomplish this production with this many people in it and keep it moving. He really is an amazing person. And—and he has confidence in me!"

Paul expanded Scott's world. No longer book-centered, it became people-centered. Paul was the role model he had been searching for, wanting so much to please him, but also learning the reality of all human relationships: imperfection. He was impressed with Paul's love of drama and its use as an expression of faith. This influence transcended his high school days and Guatemala, and reached into the life he would live as an adult. Theater lighting and design became a passion, but, hopefully, he will never forget that the true light comes from the SON.

> *I will be a Father to you,*
> *and you will be my sons and daughters,*
> *says the Lord Almighty.*
>
> 2 Corinthians 6:18

CHAPTER 37

The Long Shot

"Hey, Sharon, what college are you applying to?"

"What college do you want to go to, Dave?"

"Have you taken the SAT's yet? How did you do? Bummer!"

Senior questions, senior anxieties, and senior pressures permeated the hallways of the high school. A career day was planned for the following week. In the States, this usually involved representatives from various colleges and universities talking to the students about college choices, college applications, financial aid, and other important "senior issues." But a small mission school in Guatemala could only attract one lone die-hard to come to Career Day. This brave soul was Mr. Dave Morley from Westmont Christian College in Santa Barbara, California. He would single-handedly field all the questions, concerns, anxieties, and pleas of both students and parents for one solid week. Poor man!

On Monday Mr. Morley arrived on campus. The seniors' schedules were changed to accommodate a series of lectures and discussions on COLLEGE APPLICATION. The corridors were astir. Questions were flying.

But life in the elementary wing was barely affected by the "happenings" in the upper wing. On Thursday, I was surprised to bump into Mr. Morley in the teachers' lounge. He was enjoying a cup of coffee and a rare moment of solitude.

"Welcome to CAG," I offered, breaking an awkward silence.

"Thank you," he replied. "I have been enjoying the school and the pleasant surroundings very much. The seniors I've met are quite remarkable."

"Ah!" I laughed. "One of those 'remarkable' seniors is my son."

"Really? What is his name?" he asked.

"Scott," I readily volunteered.

"Where does he want to go to college?" he inquired politely.

I hesitated, not sure how my next words would come across. "He wants to go to Princeton. It's a long shot, I know. Probably a pipe

211

dream. If we had been in the States for his senior year he might have had a chance of getting in but from here—a small mission school in Central America!—the likelihood seems very remote."

"Has he sent in any applications?" he prodded.

"Yes, to Princeton and to one other college."

"What were his SAT scores?" he persisted.

"They were pretty good," trying to let just a tinge of pride escape. "He got 780 in verbal and 790 in math for a total of 1570. He also got 800 on the Physics achievement, 800 in math achievement and 760 in Spanish achievement." They were near perfect scores.

It was his turn to pause for a minute. "Those are excellent numbers," he said after analyzing the information. "Is your son the one leading the music in chapel today?"

"Yup, that's him, with Dave and Chris. He does music ministry. He's also in student government and drama," I added, succumbing to an urge to boast.

"Yes, I know who your son is. His teachers have mentioned him. Are there any other things he's done or accomplishments?"

Watch out! The gates to this proud mother's tongue had just been unleashed. Award after award and honor after honor tumbled out, culminating with the National Science Symposium when he was thirteen years old, and then the International Science Symposium in London after that.

"Do you have any documentation of this?" he asked.

"I have the New York Times newspaper article and other clippings about his accomplishments," I offered.

"Could you get copies of them together for me?"

"Yes, easily," I said. "I brought them down to Guatemala, and we've got a copier here at school. Why do you want them?" I asked.

He was writing notes on a piece of paper, but lifted his head to look at me. "I happen to know Fred Hargadon very well. Fred is the Dean of Admission at Princeton. We have been friends for a long time. So if you get that packet together for me I will talk to him personally about your son."

Dumbfounded, I just stared at him, my mouth gaping, hardly believing what just was said. Of all the people that would come to this little school, God had sent a close friend of Dean Hargadon.

"Do you have any other questions?" he asked, confused by my lack of response. "I will be leaving tomorrow afternoon to return to California. Can you have the copies ready by then?"

"Oh, yes," I finally responded, enthusiastically. "I'm sure of it! Thank you, Mr. Morley!"

Two weeks later I got a phone call from Mr. Morley. "I wanted to bring you up to date," he volunteered. "A rather strange coincidence happened. Last week I attended a conference for Christian colleges here in California, and was quite surprised to see Fred Hargadon there. We started chatting and I brought up your son's name. He was interested and wanted to see some documentation. I had only been back from Guatemala a few days and so the packet you gave me was still in my briefcase. I showed it to him and he said he would look over Scott's application personally as soon as he got back to Princeton."

"That's fantastic!" I blurted out. "Thank you so much, Mr. Morley." My mind groped for better words of momentous appreciation. "Thank you," I repeated, coming up blank.

"You might be hearing from him soon," he said, just before he hung up.

My conversation with Mr. Morley took place in early November. November passed and December jingled in. Christmas was only a few days away and all the decorations had been hung. I hadn't heard from Mr. Morley or Dean Hargadon. The doubts about Scott being accepted into Princeton returned. How many students from tiny mission schools in Latin America were admitted to Princeton anyway? Not many! That much was sure! Even with Mr. Morley's help it was a long shot—a long, long shot. The Christian Academy wasn't a prestigious prep school and I was certainly not a wealthy parent or benevolent Princeton donor. Yes, chances were very slim at best!

A motorcycle was beeping outside our gate, interrupting my gloom. A delivery boy was shouting something in Spanish.

"Mom, did you order pizza for dinner tonight?" Chris asked, hopefully. Motorcycles were the preferred pizza-delivery vehicle in Guatemala.

"No, honey, I didn't," I said. "He must have the wrong address. Ask him what he wants."

Chris opened the front door, and the boy's mumbled words came through the door: "*¿Quién llama?*" Who called?

"It's not for us," he answered back emphatically. "We didn't order any pizza."

"*¿Quién llama?*" Chris heard again.

"No!" Chris said more loudly. "It's not for us. Go away!"

Scott came out of the front door as the boy repeated himself one more time.

"NO! It's not for us!" Chris shouted.

"Wait," Scott interrupted. "Chris, he's not asking who called—he's saying *telegrama,* not *quién llama.*"

"*Sí,*" said the boy, relieved to have someone understand him. "*Telegrama,*" he repeated as he stuffed the telegram in Scott's hand and pointed to a spot for him to sign. He took the signature and his motorcycle sped off down the street.

Scott opened the envelope. There was only one word in the message,

"YES!"

Underneath was Dean Hargadon's signature. Scott was going to Princeton.

God's words came back to me, when I had worried earlier about his education. "Child, I am the one who gave him his abilities and his intellect. If I gave them to him, I surely have a purpose for them. If I have a purpose for them, I will surely watch over his education and provide for him what he needs."

Was it a coincidence that Mr. Morley came to CAG for Career Day?

Was it a coincidence that Mr. Morley was a close friend of Dean Hargadon?

Was it a coincidence that he ran into Dean Hargadon at a Christian college conference?

Was it a coincidence he still had the packet in his briefcase at the conference?

No, not coincidence: the act of a loving Father. The long shot was true to its course when released from the hand of God.

> *I lift up my eyes to the hills—*
> *where does my help come from?*
> *My help comes from the* LORD,
> *the Maker of heaven and earth,*

THE LONG SHOT

He will not let your foot slip—
* he who watches over you will not slumber;*
indeed, he who watches over Israel
* will neither slumber nor sleep.*
The LORD *watches over you—*
* the* LORD *is your shade at your right hand;*
the sun will not harm you by day,
* nor the moon by night.*
The LORD *will keep you from all harm—*
* he will watch over your life;*
The LORD *will watch over your coming and going*
* both now and forevermore.*

Psalm 121

CHAPTER 38

Angels on the Trail

Scott would graduate from high school in just a few weeks. He was still so young, only sixteen. Was he ready to handle life on a college campus? So many things could happen, and I wouldn't be there to shelter him. Daily I prayed to God, wondering and worrying about who would watch over him.

It was clear that Scott was struggling too, wanting to hold onto the friendships and life here, and yet eager to begin a new chapter. A bridge, a rite of passage, seemed necessary to him as proof that he was no longer a child but a man, ready to assume a life away from his family. But what form would this transition take?

"Mom, I want to go hiking," he announced as we were returning home from school.

"Where, Scott, and with whom?" I inquired, thinking this was a planned activity with the school.

"I don't know with whom, maybe just Mr. McGuire. I want to go backpacking in the northern part of Guatemala. We'd pack light, just a sleeping bag, and live off the land for a week."

Mr. McGuire was a high school English teacher at CAG, well liked, spontaneous and a bit of a "free spirit."

"Just you and Mr. McGuire? No way, Scott! What you're suggesting is way too dangerous and neither you nor Mr. McGuire have the skill to handle such a trip."

"Mr. McGuire has gone backpacking before," defended Scott, latching more firmly onto this "back to the wilds" idea.

"Where?" I challenged.

"In the States, in a national park somewhere, I think," Scott answered.

"Scott, hiking in a protected national park is a whole lot different than hiking in the jungles of Guatemala," I said.

"How?" Scott pressed, refusing to acknowledge the obvious.

"There are guerrillas here, in case you've forgotten, who would just love to find two unprotected *gringos* asleep in the open with all their possessions free for the taking. And guerrillas, as well as bandits, have been known to kill people. Scott, it's a crazy idea and way too dangerous. No way am I going to let you go backpacking with Mr. McGuire!" With that statement the matter was closed, or so I thought.

A few days later, while we were eating supper, Scott casually mentioned that Deena, Ryan, Heather, and Heidi might go on the hike too.

"Scott, I thought we settled this. You are NOT backpacking in the jungles!" I said firmly. "And I'm quite sure that Heather and Heidi's dad won't allow them to go either. It would even be more dangerous for girls at night in the open than for boys."

"Ryan is going for sure and his parents have already said it's okay," Scott shot back. "Mr. McGuire is going even if no one else goes with him. I want to go, Mom. Please?"

"Scott, don't make this into an issue. The answer is NO," I said with finality.

Even the *thought* of him out, unprotected, in the wilds of Guatemala sent me into a major worry fit. In the past three years we had our fill of stories about *bandidos* and guerrillas. Missionaries traveling the trails in upper Guatemala were often attacked. Some were just robbed, some were beaten, and a few were even killed. Just recently a mission station had been raided and the supplies stolen. The people had escaped but only to see their home and possessions go up in flames. Women left unprotected had worse things happen. No, Guatemala was not a place where a group of young teenagers could go casually backpacking for a week.

"Mom, Mr. McGuire is planning the trip for Easter break."

"NO WAY!"

"I will need a sleeping bag and some supplies, Mom."

"Scott, are you listening? NO WAY!"

Easter break was fast approaching. Scott hadn't mentioned the trip in two weeks. But now the anticipated time was only four days away.

"Mom, the trip is still planned," Scott offered hopefully. "But there are a few changes—"

"SCOTT!" I interrupted in a voice just slightly shy of a scream.

"No, listen, Mom," he rushed, into perilous territory. "You might like the changes. We'll only be hiking over Saturday and Sunday. Mr. Townsend, Heidi and Heather's dad, will drive us to a village near Cobán, in the southern part of the Petén. We're going to hike during the day. Then he'll meet us at four in the afternoon, just before it gets dark and drive us to a lodge. We'll sleep *inside,* Mom," he continued, taking advantage of my momentary silence, "in a protected place, just like you wanted. We'll hike some on Sunday too. Then he'll drive us back to the city. Can I go? PLEASE?" he begged.

I didn't respond right away. Analyzing this information, I knew the Townsends were cautious parents and knowledgeable about the area. They'd lived here for a good fifteen or more years, and some of that was in isolated villages. If they were letting their daughters go it was definitely a positive consideration.

"You can call Mr. Townsend," Scott eagerly suggested.

"I will," I said more calmly.

"I want to go, too," Chris suddenly piped in, taking advantage of the changed mood. If there was going to be an adventure, he wanted to be included!

Early Saturday morning, the small group met in front of Mr. Townsend's house. There was Mr. McGuire and six high school students: Heidi, Heather, Deena, Ryan, Chris, and Scott, all eager for the expedition.

"Scott, Chris, come here for a minute," I called as they finished unloading their gear from the car. "I want to pray with you before you leave."

With an air of impatience, they looked at each other. I placed my hands on their shoulders. This was a common practice, one they were used to—my praying for their safety before they went somewhere. Nor were the words unusual:

"Dear Lord, watch over my boys today, and this group, as they travel and as they hike. Keep them safe and in your care. Thank you, Father. In Jesus' name I pray. Amen."

With a quick kiss, the boys darted off to join the others, most of who were already loaded into Mr. Townsend's jeep. I waved goodbye as they rattled off for a three-hour drive north.

The plan was that today they would hike on a trail Mr. Townsend had plotted on a map. They'd meander over a mountain and back down to meet Mr. Townsend at four in the afternoon. It was important to be off the mountain before the sun set at five. The plan seemed simple enough.

But not long after they'd begun, Mr. McGuire decided that the trail was too tame, not adventurous enough. Another trail looked more intriguing. The group followed into thicker terrain.

For hours they hiked, enjoying this remote area. But the sun was dipping low to the horizon and the expected road didn't appear. Instead, the jungle grew denser. The map was useless. There were no landmarks to guide them. The possibility started to sink in that they could be lost.

Up ahead, they spotted a small Indian village. As they entered the compound, twenty or so men gathered around them.

"We're lost." Scott promptly informed the men in Spanish. "Can you tell us how to get back to the main road?"

The men made no response. Their eyes coldly evaluated the group, especially the young girls.

"We're lost," Scott repeated. "Can you help us?"

Still no response, but they mumbled among themselves in a Mayan dialect.

"Do we go that way or that way to the road?" Scott tried again, pointing as he talked.

"*Sí,*" one man said.

"*¿Sí?*" Scott questioned. "*Sí,* this way, or *sí,* that way?"

"*Sí,*" the man said again. The others chuckled behind him.

An uneasy feeling moved in upon the gathering. Restless and agitated, the villagers formed a tighter ring around the group. Then the men pushed forward and surrounded Mr. McGuire. Voices shouted in the native language accusingly. Arms raised menacingly. Dark eyes focused on the young girls. The circle parted just for a moment, and the six escaped down the trail. The men's angry voices reverberated in the dark jungle shadows around them.

"We can't leave Mr. McGuire," Deena's voice pleaded.

"But we can't go back to that village, either," rationalized Ryan.

"What should we do?" a very tense and frightened voice asked in the darkening shades of evening. The full impact of their predicament hit them soundly. They were lost. They were in danger. It was almost night. And Mr. McGuire was—being held? Captive?

"Hold my hands," Heather whispered. "Let's pray."

No one challenged her and no one questioned her timing. They huddled, without a second thought, jungle leaves around them. The prayer was a desperate plea for help and protection from six very frightened youths. Their amen was a unison benediction.

As they faced the trail again, another Indian approached them from the direction opposite the village. "What is the matter?" he inquired kindly in Spanish.

"The men in the village have our friend, and they won't let him go."

"Don't worry. I will help you," the man said simply, and he strolled down the path. The village men were still shouting and waving their arms around Mr. McGuire, but as they saw the lone figure approach, their voices quieted, and the arms around Mr. McGuire dropped. The crowd parted and they viewed the newcomer with bewilderment.

"Come with me," the Indian motioned to Mr. McGuire, who gladly chose to follow, running, sliding, and skidding down the muddy jungle pass to join the six others. No one from the village followed.

"Where do we go?" Scott asked. "We don't know how to get back to the main road and it's dark now. What should we do?"

"Keep going," the Indian said calmly. "You will be safe."

Frightened and uncertain, they proceeded on their ordeal. The ground was so muddy, only a few steps could be taken before one of the group would slip and fall, slowing the progress. Over and over they fell. Their clothes were crusted in mire. The night had become so black they couldn't even see the person ahead of them. Only their tense voices joined them. Chris had a small pack of matches and whenever they weren't sure if they were still on the trail, he would light just one to check.

"There are sink holes in this area," Ryan warned ominously.

"What are sink holes?" Heather asked.

"Holes that fall into limestone caves way below the surface. If you trip into one, you'd never be able to get out again. No one would even know where you were," he explained.

"I didn't need to know that!" Heather moaned.

"We should be okay if we stay on the trail," he reasoned.

"But we're not even sure we're on the trail," Heidi complained. "Chris, light another match."

"We're at a junction of two paths," Scott, who was in the lead, announced. "I don't know which way to go. This way?"

"You're okay," the Indian said reassuringly. "Keep going."

A little further down the way they came to another junction. "Which way? This way?" asked Scott, again, with tension in his voice.

"You're okay," the Indian repeated. "Keep going."

221

At each fork the Indian would repeat those words, "You're okay, keep going," and his reassuring voice encouraged them.

Hour after hour the group fell and slid and stumbled down the invisible jungle path, along a precipice they could only imagine, in a direction they only hoped was right. The Indian never left Scott's side.

His presence, though calming, was puzzling. There was no reason for him to walk hours out of his way just for a group of lost Americans, unless he expected a large payment at the end.

"That must be the reason," concluded Ryan. "He wants us to pay him something when we get to the road—*if* we get to the road."

"I have no problem paying him if he gets us to the road," volunteered Chris.

"How much money do we have among us?" asked Scott.

"Probably about a hundred quetzals," Ryan figured. "I think that will do."

"I'd be glad to give him all the money I had," Chris again offered.

The money passed among them as they trudged further down the path.

About ten o'clock at night the jungle thinned and they emerged from the pitch-black jungle. A few hundred feet ahead was a road!

"We've made it," Chris sighed to himself. "We've made it!" he repeated louder.

"Thank you, Lord," acknowledged Heather.

"The money!" Ryan said. "Scott, give the Indian the money."

Scott turned to thank the man for his help. He was ready to give him more than a hundred quetzals. But the Indian wasn't there.

"Where did he go?" questioned Scott.

"Where did who go?" asked Deena.

"The Indian, the one who led us down the trail," he explained.

"One?" queried Deena.

"Yes, the one in front with me," repeated Scott.

"Then there were two," Deena mused slowly. "There was also one behind me, following us."

Their eyes searched the surrounding terrain, looking for either of the two guides but there was no sign of them, anywhere, only stillness and peace.

Two headlights appeared down the road.

"Quick!" said Heather. "Let's flag the car down!"

Her words didn't need repeating. The group was already running towards the road, hands waving and voices shouting. The car pulled to the shoulder.

"I've been searching for you all night! Where have you been?" the familiar voice inside cried out. Mr. Townsend jumped out and hugged his daughters, relieved and exhausted. The very tired and muddy band scrambled into the jeep, and with grateful hearts they headed for shelter and safety.

My sons were safe. All the children were safe. Were they angels that watched over the small group, protecting them on the dangerous trail, or just men sent by God? It didn't matter. My children had been in danger and God had protected them. The simple prayer prayed in the morning was faithfully answered. I didn't even know of their difficulty until the next day and yet God lovingly watched over them.

My fears and worries about Scott's safety in college seemed insignificant now. Who would watch over him so far away from home? God had just shown me the answer. He would be with him always.

> *The angel of the* LORD *encamps*
> *around those who fear him,*
> *and he delivers them.*
> *Taste and see that the* LORD *is good;*
> *blessed is the man who takes refuge in him.*   Psalm 34:7–8

CHAPTER 39

A Degree in Humanity

May, 1993: high school graduation—a day that is hard to imagine ever arriving for a young mother with a baby in her arms. How did my young son get to be so tall? When did his little boy features lose their softness and take on the ruggedness of manhood? How did it happen so fast?

Scott stood at a distance from me with his blue graduation robe loosely over his shoulders. He was casually talking with the other seniors under the canopied tent on the grounds of the Antigua Hotel. The hot tropical sun was beating unmercifully on them. His fingers lightly touched the medallion around his neck, worn as the valedictorian of his class. How much he had changed in these three years...

The younger students in the school orchestra tuned their instruments. A signal was given and the procession of flags began: United States, Canada, New Zealand, Mexico, and Guatemala—a flag for each country the graduates represented. Then the graduating class of seventeen seniors walked down the aisle to the slightly-off rendition of *Pomp and Circumstance*. My eyes were only on Scott.

I know I should have been overcome with a feeling of pride and joy on this special occasion, but in truth, I was caught in an eddy of intense sorrow. Maybe it was a premonition, or just the gut instinct that told me this was the last time Scott would be my "child," living under my roof, enjoying daily activities and life with me. Today would mark that permanent separation where our lives would diverge. "Home" would no longer be a residence but merely a place to visit for a day or so, or maybe a week. I had been trying to let go but every fiber in me wanted to hold onto him: my child, my son. He was so young and, to me, so naïve and unprepared to take on the world alone. God had assured me He would watch over him, but I knew only too well that didn't mean Scott would be immune to hurt and disappointment—all the things I so desperately wanted to protect him from.

Tears rolled down my cheeks as I watched him take his place behind the podium and begin his valedictorian speech. He looked all around him, at his fellow students, at the teachers, and lastly, at me in the audience. His first words were not praises for his teachers, or for the academic strengths of CAG, or for the school propelling him to greater intellectual achievements. Those things, in truth, he had before he even came to the Christian Academy of Guatemala. But what he didn't have was an appreciation for how our relationship to God was expressed with the people around us. The school showed him service, fellowship, worship, friendship, vision, and the truths of God worked out on the daily level of humanity. CAG connected him to people. He could no longer be happy with just his books and computer. He was a personality now, tied to other personalities, sometimes leading, sometimes following, sometimes learning, and sometimes teaching. God knew what type of "education" Scott needed and in his sovereignty supplied it through CAG. Scott thanked his teachers and the school for this gift that was of more value than all the academic honors the world could grant.

The applause after his speech resounded in my ears. Yes, God, you are sovereign. You will take care of him as he leaves me to go to Princeton University, such a contrast to this humble little school. But please, though, also take care of my "mother's heart" that longs so dearly to always hold him in my arms.

> *Why are you downcast, O my soul?*
> *Why so disturbed within me?*
> *Put your hope in God,*
> *for I will yet praise him,*
> *my Savior and my God.*

Psalm 43:5

CHAPTER 40

Final Packing

A week later Scott and Chris left on a missions trip to Canada with a dozen other kids from CAG. It was a drama tour sponsored by Wycliffe missions. The feature was a play titled, *Tolo, Son of the Volcano*. Chris had the lead as Tolo, a Guatemalan peasant, who found truth in God's word. Scott played the the part of Marcos, a revolutionary, who was ready to battle against the injustices of the world. God, to him, was a nonentity, a crutch for the weak. At the end of the play Chris "died" in Scott's arms and Scott's character realizes the Truth that God's salvation is real and attainable.

The play was to tour all through Canada and New England, playing in churches, auditoriums, fields, and park gazebos. They would even appear on Canadian television. I did not expect the boys to be under "my roof" again until August.

So...I was left alone in Guatemala to finish selling off the household items and pack up all the things we needed for our return to the States. My primary concern, however, was a job. Many letters of inquiry and résumés had been sent to U.S. school districts. Not one response had come back. My trust in God was evaporating into panic again. The same nagging and persistent question rattled in my head as it did five years earlier: WOULD GOD PROVIDE? This concern took on familiar aspects such as: Where would I live? What shape would my house be in? Would my car still run? And then new concerns were added such as: Where would Chris go to school? How would I meet all the expenses waiting for me when I stepped off the plane? How would I pay my mortgage bills? How would I pay Princeton tuition bills? How would I even pay for food until September when I would start teaching again—*if* I started teaching again? Anxious and panicky thoughts spiraled in my head.

I made my requests known to the Lord frequently—*very* frequently! "Lord," I would pray urgently, "I *need* a job at the salary level I left three years ago. I *need* Scott's tuition bills met and my mortgage bills met. I want a good high school for Chris, where he won't have to worry about getting beat up. And—oh, if possible, Lord," I tentatively added, "I would like a job in a school where your name could enter through the door as well."

The letters I sent to the States concerning jobs seemed to be swallowed in a void. No responses came back. No nibbles, no questions, NOTHING!

"God," I prayed, "What about a job? God, I *need* a teaching job and it's already the end of June." My voice raised in intensity, "God, are you hearing me? *I need a job!*"

Thoughts raced through my mind: how could I make God hear me? Impudently I wondered how one could control the Almighty. "Lord," I implored one night, "If I had a thousand people praying on my behalf for a job, would you hear me? God, if I fasted for a week, or maybe two weeks, would you hear me? Lord, do you hear me if it's just my small voice pleading beside my bed? God, how do I make you respond? God, please answer me: what direction am I to go in from here? *Please* answer me!"

The room echoed my questions but responded in silence.

In my Bible reading that night, I read Psalm 32:

. . . You are my hiding place;
you will protect me from trouble
and surround me with songs of deliverance.

I will instruct you and teach you
in the way you should go;
I will counsel you and watch over you.
Do not be like the horse or the mule,
which have no understanding
but must be controlled by bit and bridle
or they will not come to you.
Many are the woes of the wicked,
but the LORD*'s unfailing love*
surrounds the man who trusts in him.
Rejoice in the LORD *and be glad, you righteous;*
sing, all you who are upright in heart!

Instead of finding comfort in God's words, I tore at the page and ripped it. I wept in frustration, "God, how can I rejoice when I am frightened? Your promises of unfailing love 'surrounds the man who trusts'! But God, I stumble on trust every time! I am the horse and the mule that has no understanding! Lord, I *want* you to instruct me and guide me in where I should go. I beg to hear your counsel. But only your silence surrounds me and it frightens me."

The house in Guatemala was emptied. All our things were in suitcases and boxes. There was no farewell committee. Everyone else had already left for the summer. Leaving is so lonely. Memories swirl in a panorama of countless events and people. Shadows were already replacing the vibrant colors and images that had surrounded me for three years in Guatemala.

As I sat in the airport waiting for my plane to be called I tried to grasp God's plan. "God," I questioned again, "Have I accomplished your mission? Have I done what you wanted? Have I learned the eternal truth you wanted to reveal to me? I feel so defeated and uncertain. Why can't I trust? Why do my anxious thoughts defeat me every time? I stayed, Lord, the extra years, to learn your nature—to learn you can be trusted, but your silence has confounded me."

> *I cried out to God for help;*
> *I cried out to God to hear me.*
> *When I was in distress, I sought the Lord;*
> *at night I stretched out untiring hands*
> *and my soul refused to be comforted.*
> *I remembered you, O God, and I groaned;*
> *I mused and my spirit grew faint.*   Psalm 77:1–3

"Flight 164, now boarding. Destination: Miami, Florida, U.S.A."

CHAPTER 41

Unseen Footprints

. . . and my soul refused to be comforted. . .   Psalm 77:2

Can God be trusted? Will He provide? I was out on a limb with no one else and no other resources left to depend on but God; No safety nets under me: no parents, no job, no income, nothing. "But," the thought crept in, "maybe—just maybe, that was exactly where He wanted me to be." I knew that one way or the other the answer to my questions would be decisively revealed in the next two months.

I pleaded for God's comfort, and knew Psalm 77 did not end where my thoughts were marooned. It went on:

> *Then I thought, "To this I will appeal:*
> *the years of the right hand of the Most High."*
> *I will remember the deeds of the* LORD;
> *yes, I will remember your miracles of long ago.*
> *I will meditate on all your works*
> *and consider all your mighty deeds. . .*
> *though your footprints were not seen,*
> *You led your people like a flock.*

Yes, Lord, you provided in the past. I do remember what you did before. "Please Lord," I prayed, "let me follow and trust in the footprints that I don't see."

In my devotions I read:

> *"I tell you the truth," Jesus replied, "no one who has left home or brothers or sisters or mother or father or children or fields for me and the gospel will fail to receive a hundred times as much in this present age. . . ."*   Mark 10:29–30

As I read that, it struck me as an awesome promise. But my anxiety level was off the scales. TRUST! Why can't I trust?

It was late on a hot July day that I reentered my house after a three-year absence. It was bare and forlorn. Scott and Chris were not beside me to exuberantly explore the premises. A huge hole in the living room wall confirmed my grim expectations. But besides a bent garage door, the rest appeared okay. The car was covered with three years worth of dirt and grime. But after a new battery was installed it worked just fine. Amazing!

Job hunting was intense. There were jobs but with salaries at a third of what I needed to live on. I knew exactly what salary I needed to make the ends meet, and just meet. I had presented God with this amount numerous times. "Are you listening?" I challenged.

In the beginning of August I was offered a job. The salary was exactly what I had prayed for, but it was not in the setting I expected: the position was as a teacher in the resource room at an Orthodox Jewish day school. I questioned the Lord, "Is this where you want me? What use could I be for you there?"

Oswald Chambers in *My Utmost For His Highest* spoke God's wry answer:

August 10

... Notice God's unutterable waste of saints, according to the judgment of the world. God plants His saints in the most useless places. We say—God intends me to be here because I am so useful. Jesus never estimated His life along the line of the greatest use. God put His saints where they will glorify Him, and we are no judges at all of where that is.

I remembered when we first arrived in Honduras, I had arrogantly declared to the Lord, "Look God, what I am doing for you!" And he quickly replied, "No, child, look what I am doing for you!" Again his purposes and plans were invisible to me but I was to trust and glorify Him. The salary was exactly what I had prayed for, and, with a chuckle, I remembered the added request: "Lord, if possible, it would be nice if your name could go through the door with me, too." Yes, I realized, His name, the Jewish equivalent *Hashem, would* go through the door with me. Next time I will make sure to include Jesus's name in my prayer, I smiled. But praise God, and Jesus! I had a job!

Scott and Chris returned before the end of the month. They were filled with marvelous tales of God's workings all across Canada. Scott immediately began preparations for college. So many things needed to be unpacked and then packed again. Boxes and boxes were brought out of storage. Strangely, though, the things unpacked belonged to little boys: toys, books, room decorations, even winter clothes in much smaller sizes. But who stood before me now were almost men.

An intense time warp engulfed me. Surely it was only yesterday I had packed away these things so carefully, these toys and warm clothes for my little boys.

They'd need them, I remembered thinking, when we got back. Where were those little boys? How could they have grown up on me so quickly? And Scott was leaving for college!

Can time be stopped, God? Just for a little while longer? I want to see my sons play on the swing again, and ride their bikes like the wind down the street. I want to see them asleep in their beds, so young and innocent, just one more time, and kiss them on their foreheads all sweaty from play.

"Mom, why are you crying?" Scott asked softly standing almost six feet tall before me.

I was holding a boy's size twelve pants in my hand. "You wore these just before we left. Look at you, Scott! You couldn't even get your foot in them now," I tried to smile. My little boys had grown up. And—in spite of the fact I wish I could have held on to my little men a bit longer—I was proud of who stood before me now.

Two weeks later I took Scott to Princeton for freshman orientation. He was only 16, but with the Lord watching over him I felt confident he'd be okay. His face was glowing with excitement as he joined the others in his class that warm day.

Chris still needed to be re-enrolled into high school. I had major concerns about the high school in town; it was not the environment I wanted for him. However—in a casual conversation with a friend, I found out a new "magnet school" had just been started on the Brookdale Community College campus. It was part of the county public school system but specifically for high-achieving students with an interest in technology. Acceptance was stiff and it was almost certain that the quota of students from Monmouth County had already been filled. Even so, I called the principal of High Technology High School. It was a long shot. Would Chris qualify? Would there be a space for him?

God must have shaken his head in bewilderment as I so slowly grasped Trust. Should I have been surprised when the principal in-

formed me there had just been a cancellation? A student in the sopho-
more class had decided just that morning not to go to High Tech, and
so: there was a spot open. And should I have been surprised when
Chris's grades and achievement scores just happen to meet the requirements? Praise God! Chris was accepted and God HAD heard
my concerns.

> *Do not be anxious about anything, but in everything, by*
> *prayer and petition, with thanksgiving, present your re-*
> *quests to God. And the peace of God, which transcends*
> *all understanding, will guard your hearts and your minds*
> *in Christ Jesus.*   Philippians 4:6–7

My challenge to God had been, WOULD YOU PROVIDE?
COULD I TRUST YOU? I had put trust on the line when I stayed
two more years in Guatemala and returned with no safety net or support system but God. In the world's terms, imagine the absurdity of
having nothing to depend on but God. In spiritual terms, imagine the
absurdity of saying I had nothing to depend on but God—and still
worrying!

Would he take care of my house that had almost gone into foreclo-
sure? The answer was now in: YES!

Would he provide a job for me, with the salary I needed to pay my
monthly expenses? The answer was YES, even with a chuckle as I
heard the name "Hashem" daily in the halls of the school.

Would he provide for Scott's education? Again the answer was
YES, abundantly YES, in one of the country's leading universities. His
yearly tuition was almost entirely paid for in grants and scholarships.
Scott adapted to campus life quickly and became actively involved in
theater and in the Princeton Evangelical Fellowship. His grades were
outstanding.

And Chris? Would he go to a high school where he wouldn't have
to worry about getting beat up or intimidated? The answer was YES,
abundantly, graciously YES, in the fifth-best-ranked high school in
New Jersey. He excelled in academics and in leadership. He started a
chapter of the Fellowship for Christian Athletes and graduated fourth
in his class.

> *...and my soul refused to be comforted...*
> *Then I thought, "To this I will appeal:*

234

> *the years of the right hand of the Most High."*
> *I will remember the deeds of the* LORD*;*
> *yes, I will remember your miracles of long ago.*
> *I will meditate on all your works*
> *and consider all your mighty deeds...*
> *though your footprints were not seen,*
> *You led your people like a flock.*　　　　　Psalm 77

This was the ending of the psalm that my heart had been confounded on. This was *Jehovah Jireh,* God the provider. All my fears were as vapors in His hands. His invisible footprints were there all along.

Would I have picked this path on my own? The dreams and expectations I had as a young bride never even imagined divorce, full-time employment, little boys without a daddy, jungles, guns, scorpions and snakes, house foreclosures, or heartache and fear. No, I'm quite sure the path I would have chosen for myself would have been painted from a different palette.

As I pondered the events of my life, I realized that looking ahead, down the corridor of time, God's footprints seemed invisible. But Faith and Trust were the arrows. Now looking backwards, His footprints are plain and from His palette the face of Jesus is outlined in the path.

On His course I learned that when my world collapsed, I could see His world more clearly. When my little boys were afraid of big monsters, God showed them He was even bigger. When there was no real daddy's hand to hold on to, God showed my boys His hand. When I was afraid of jungles and fighting, He taught me peace. When I almost lost my house, He taught me thanksgiving. In fire and bombs He taught me protection. Compassion and love are the guard rails on His trail. And TRUST is the name of the road.

> *Trust in the* LORD *with all your heart*
> *and lean not on your own understanding;*
> *in all your ways acknowledge him,*
> *and he will make your paths straight.*　　　　　Proverbs 3:5–7

Though your foot prints are invisible, I will follow you in trust. In thanksgiving I will glorify your Name all the days of my life.

AMEN!

The Hand of God

It has been 22 years since my sons and I returned to the U.S. from Guatemala. Many who have read my story have asked if there was a sequel. Life has a way of continuing but never on the path one expects.

When we returned from Guatemala, Scott entered Princeton University. He was only 16 years old and hadn't even gotten his driver's license yet. Four years later he graduated with honors with a degree in electrical engineering and accepted a generous research assistantship from M.I.T. While attending M.I.T he met his wife-to-be, Jessica, who already had her masters in computer science and engineering from M.I.T. When he first introduced me to her, he used the Boston expression "wicked smart" to describe her and it is has proved to be very appropriate. Scott graduated from M.I.T. with his PhD in Computer Engineering. His first job was with One Laptop per Child, a non-profit aiming to empower and educate the children of developing countries by providing one connected laptop to every school-age child. He was able to use his Spanish as he worked with deployments in South America. Currently he works as a Senior Software Engineer for the Wikimedia Foundation, maintaining and enhancing the software for Wikipedia and other public resources. His wife Jessica works for Google. Scott and Jessica were married in 2011 in Hawaii, where Jessica was raised. In 2012 their first child Zachary was born and in 2015 my youngest grandchild, Adalynn, was born. Scott and Jessica live in Boston, Massachusetts.

After returning from Guatemala Chris entered High Technology High School, a "magnet" school. He then enrolled at Rutgers University where he majored in Biology and met his wife-to-be, Kimberly. After graduation he was accepted to the University of Medicine and Dentistry of New Jersey. He had a residency in radiology at the Hospital of St. Raphael in New Haven, Connecticut and a fellowship from Yale University. He currently works as a radiologist for Women's Imaging in Princeton, New Jersey. Kim received her pharmaceutical doctorate. They were married in 2004, and my first grandchild, Tyler, was born in 2007. In 2009 Alexis was born, followed by Allison in 2012 and, finally, little Jackson in 2014. That gives me a total of six beautiful and healthy grandchildren, who I adore.

When I returned from Guatemala, I worked ten years in an Orthodox Jewish day school. I attributed that to God's unique sense of humor. I taught learning-disabled children and came to appreciate the Jewish roots of Christianity. A sequel to this book would surely contain stories from this period of my life: the Kosher microwave, the Purim Easter basket, and my Jewish mission field.

Life as a teacher, Sunday School teacher, and mother (now to college-age boys) was reassuringly familiar. But the next part of my life's story seemed lifted from the Chronicles of Narnia: the children, calmly sitting in a train station, whisked suddenly into another dimension, another life and another identify.

In 2000 I met and married a pastor. His wife had died of ovarian cancer and he had a twelve-year-old daughter. My new church knew little about my previous life or my sons. I was now a pastor's wife and a mother of a young teenage girl. Even my teaching job had changed: I was now a Learning Disabilities Teacher/Consultant on the Child Study Team in the public school system, diagnosing children with learning disabilities.

They were good years. I loved my husband and my beautiful stepdaughter. Life was filled with activity: I led the women's ministry, the children's ministry, and Bible studies. Together we led short-term mission trips to Roatán, Honduras and to Eleuthera in the Bahamas. My husband was a good pastor and the church grew. But as quickly as this segment of my life began, it came to an abrupt ending in 2013 in one of the saddest and most difficult periods in my life. As before I challenged God with my questions and He has continued to teach me trust. I am truly thankful for his patience.

And now I'm just beginning another section of the book of my life, with more pages to fill with adventures. I have recently retired after 40 years of teaching. What the Lord has in store for me now is a complete unknown. As I wrote in the previous chapter, when looking backwards His footprints are plain and the face of Jesus is outlined in the path. But when we're looking ahead the footsteps of God can be invisible—we must follow the arrows of Faith and Trust. I am so thankful for the path in life I have traveled and with the Lord as my constant companion. I am thankful for the joys as well as the sorrows.

In all things I give thanks to the Lord.

Minnie Louise Haskins wrote in her famous poem, "God Knows":

And I said to the man who stood at the gate of the year:
"Give me a light that I may tread safely into the unknown."
And he replied:
"Go out into the darkness and put your hand into the Hand of God.
That shall be to you better than light and safer than a known way."

So I will travel ahead, with my hand in the hand of God, rejoicing in all he has shown me and in all that is yet to come. He is truly faithful.

Colophon

This book was typeset by C. Scott Ananian using the LaTeX
typesetting system created by Leslie Lamport and the `memoir` class
of Peter Wilson. The body text is set 10/12pt on a 23pc measure in
Adobe Times-Roman and Helvetica.

Made in the USA
Columbia, SC
17 January 2018